# CHRISTMAS POPS

## CONTENTS

— PIANO LEVEL —
EARLY INTERMEDIATE/INTERMEDIATE
(HLSPL LEVEL 4-5)

ISBN 978-0-634-08076-0

Hal•Leonard®
CORPORATION

7777 W. BLUEMOUND RD. P.O. BOX 13819 MILWAUKEE, WI 53213

Visit Hal Leonard Online at
**www.halleonard.com**
Visit Phillip at
**www.phillipkeveren.com**

# BECAUSE IT'S CHRISTMAS
## (For All the Children)

Music by BARRY MANILOW
Lyric by BRUCE SUSSMAN and JACK FELDMAN
Arranged by Phillip Keveren

**Slow Ballad**

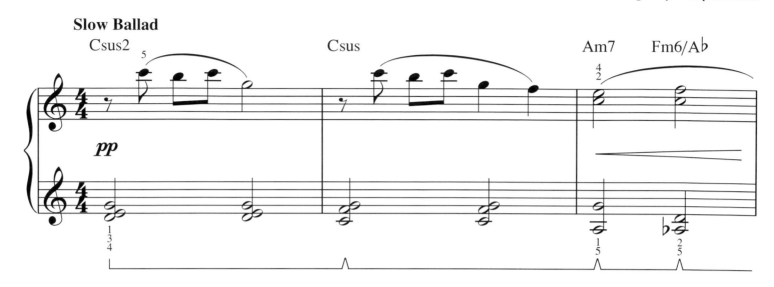

To-night the stars shine for the chil - dren,
To-night be-longs to all the chil - dren,

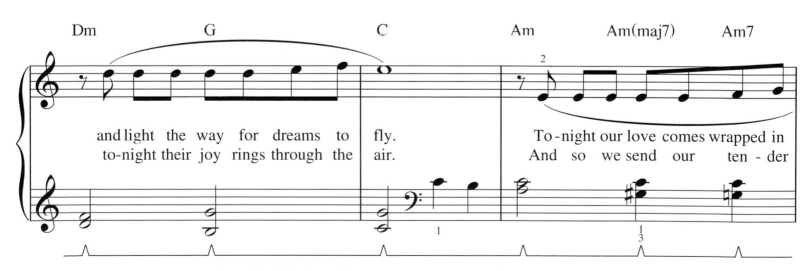

and light the way for dreams to fly.
to-night their joy rings through the air.

To-night our love comes wrapped in
And so we send our ten - der

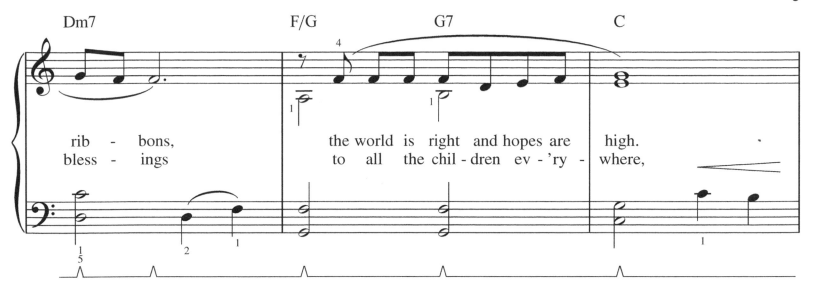

rib - bons,
bless - ings

the world is right and hopes are high.
to all the chil - dren ev - 'ry - where,

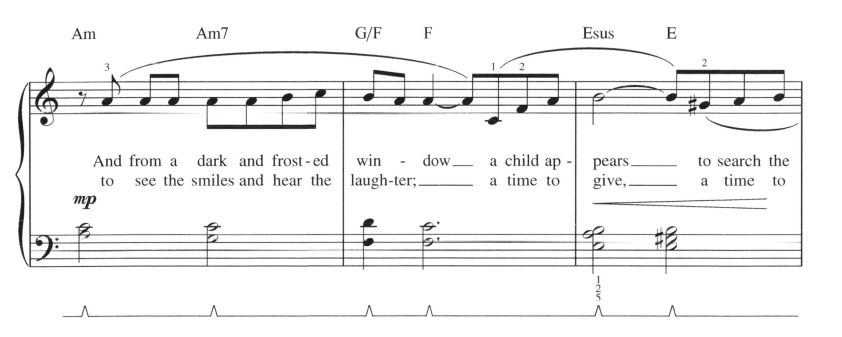

And from a dark and frost - ed win - dow___ a child ap - pears___ to search the
to see the smiles and hear the laugh - ter;___ a time to give,___ a time to

*mp*

sky,
share,

be - cause it's
be - cause it's

Christ - mas,

be - cause it's

Christ - mas.

*mf*

*dim.*

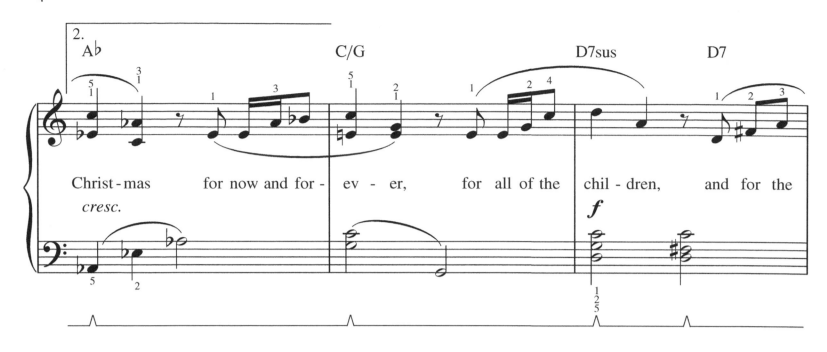

Christ-mas      for now and for - ev - er,      for all of the  chil - dren,      and for the

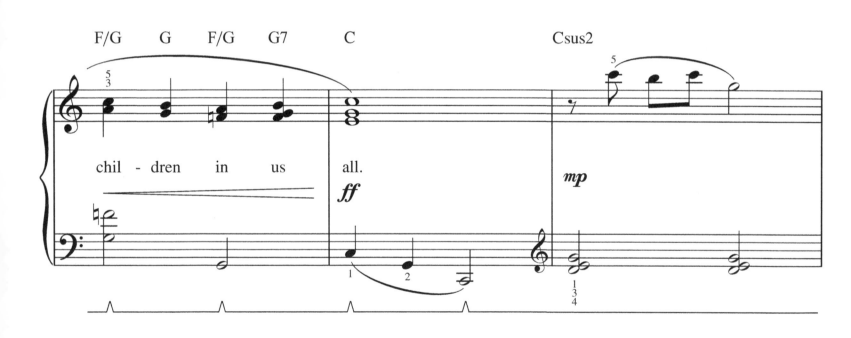

chil - dren  in  us  all.

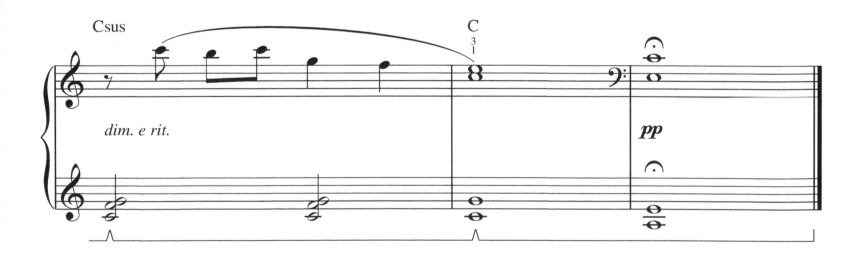

# BLUE CHRISTMAS

Words and Music by BILLY HAYES
and JAY JOHNSON
Arranged by Phillip Keveren

**Moderately bright**

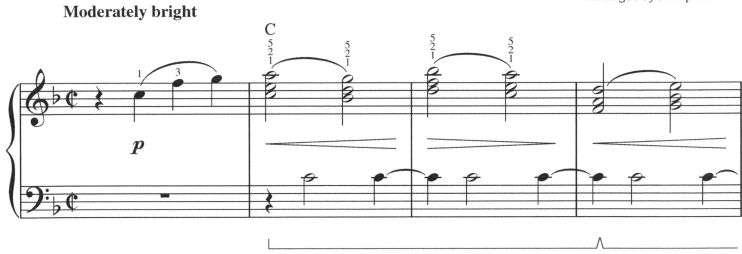

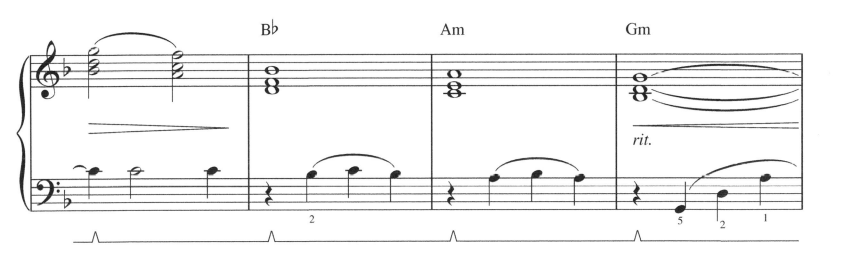

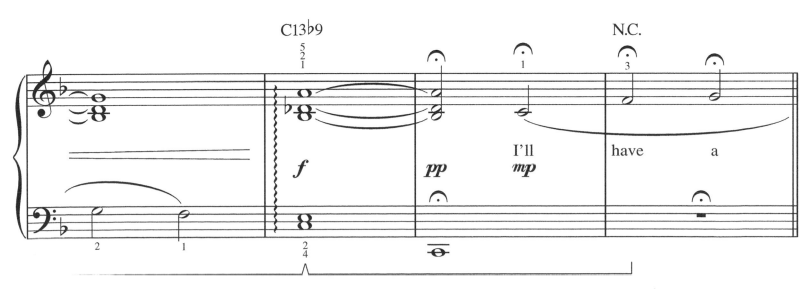

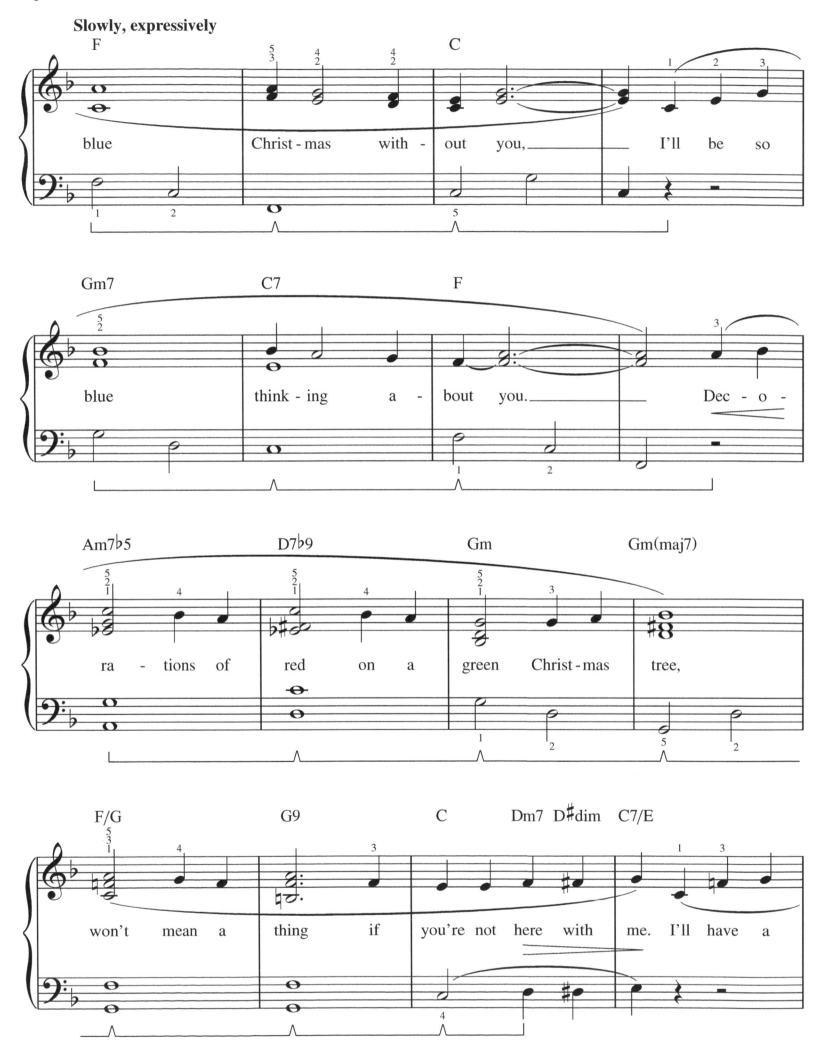

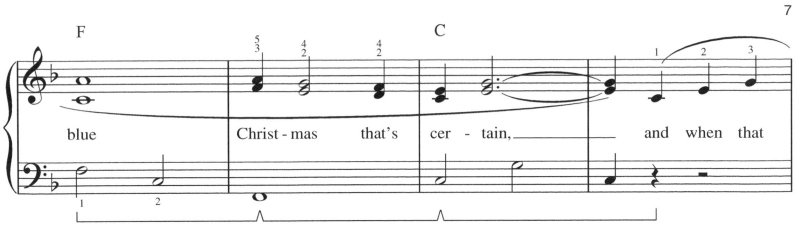

blue        Christ - mas  that's  cer - tain,_____        and when that

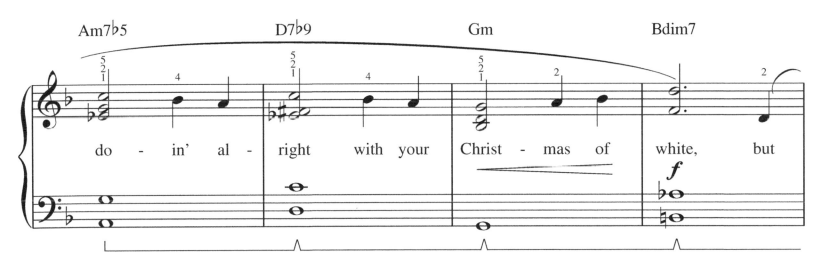

blue        heart - ache  starts  hurt - in'_____        you'll be

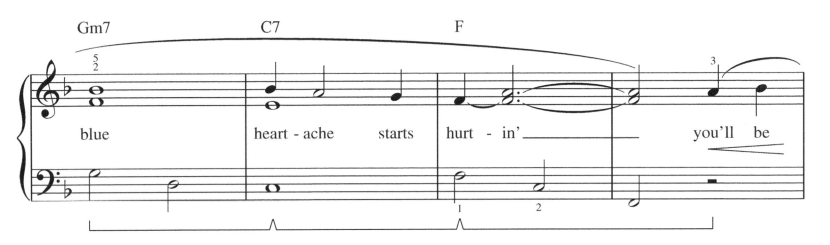

do - in' al - right  with your  Christ - mas of  white,  but

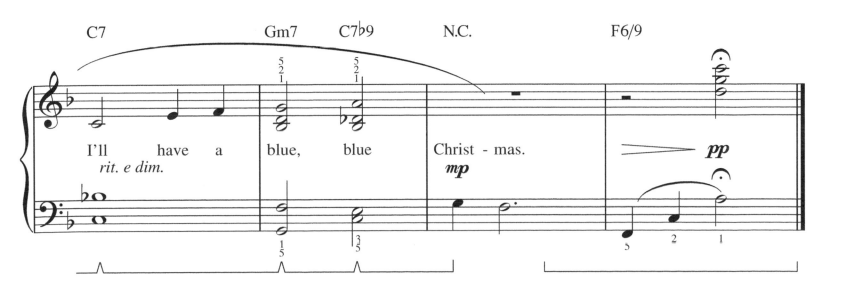

I'll    have    a    blue,    blue    Christ - mas.
*rit. e dim.*

# THE CHRISTMAS SONG
## (Chestnuts Roasting on an Open Fire)

Music and Lyric by MEL TORME
and ROBERT WELLS
Arranged by Phillip Keveren

**Slowly, warmly**

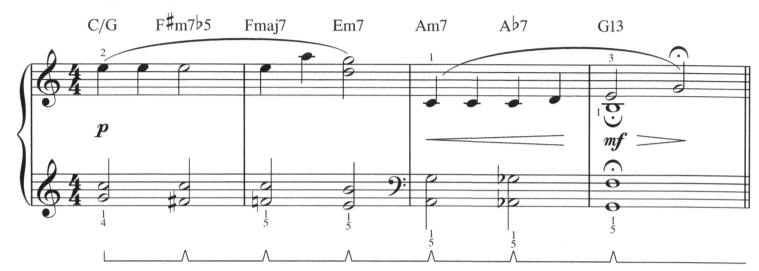

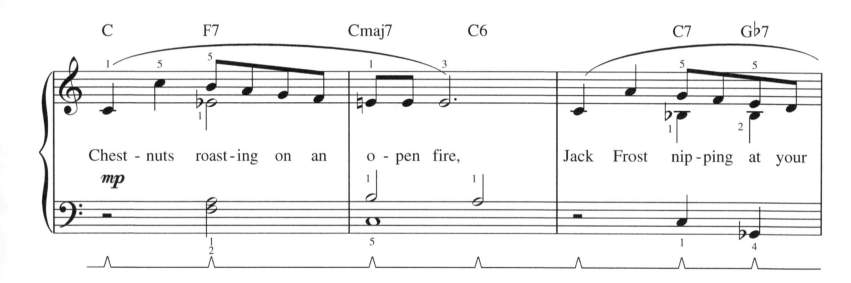

Chest-nuts roast-ing on an o-pen fire, Jack Frost nip-ping at your

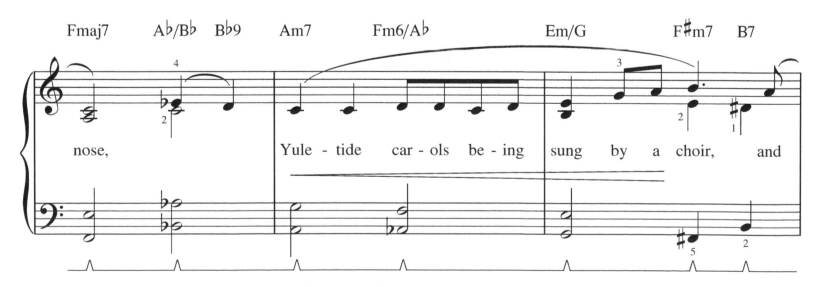

nose, Yule-tide car-ols be-ing sung by a choir, and

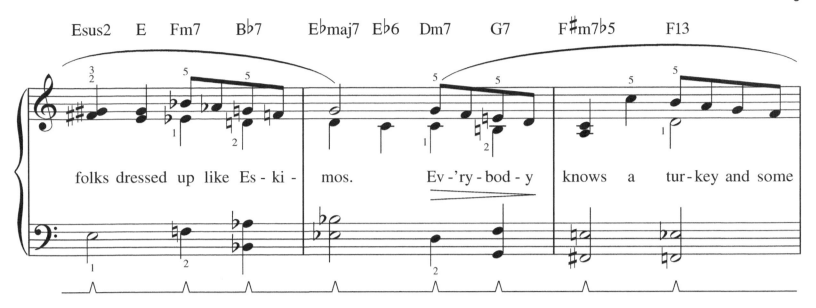

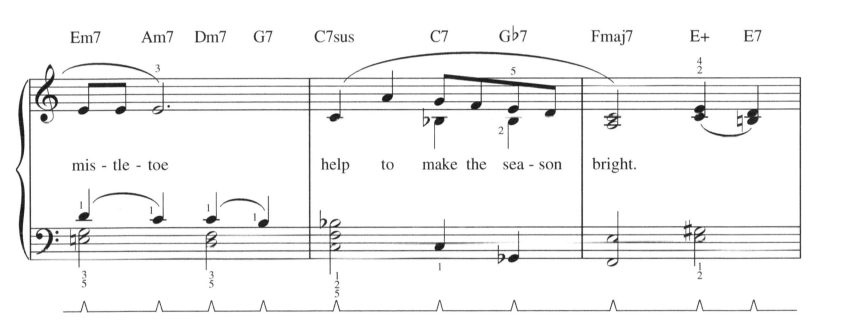

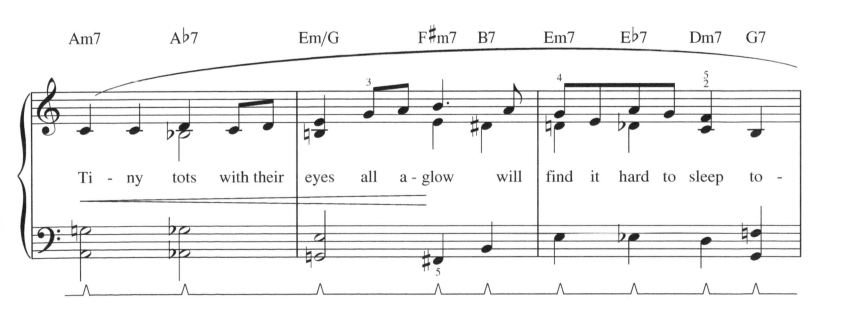

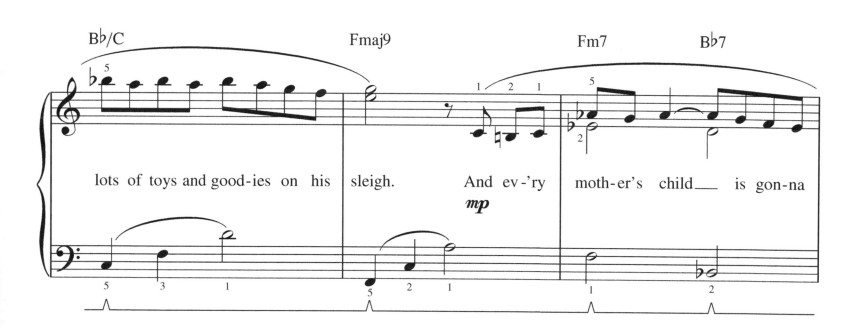

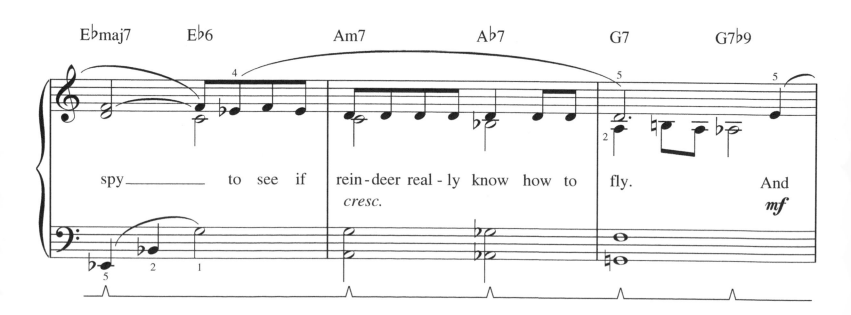

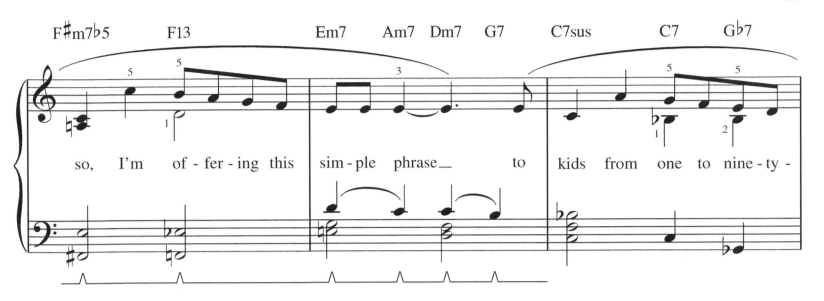

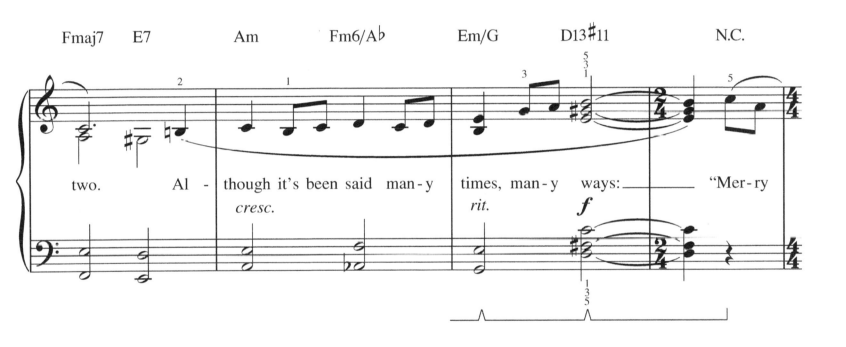

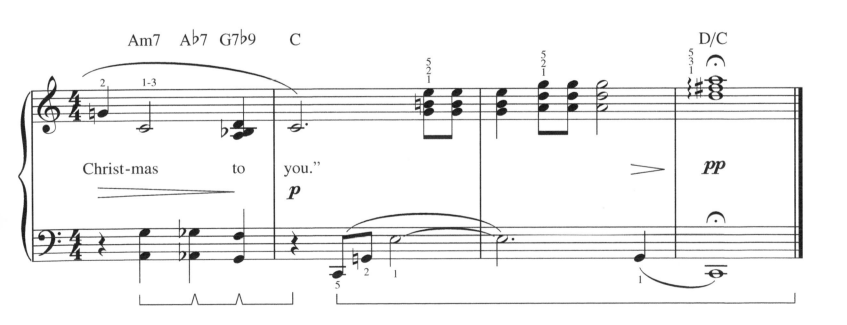

# CHRISTMAS TIME IS HERE

### from A CHARLIE BROWN CHRISTMAS

Words by LEE MENDELSON
Music by VINCE GUARALDI
Arranged by Phillip Keveren

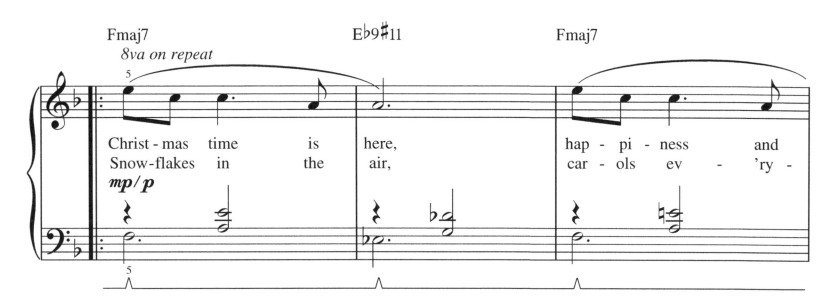

Christ - mas time is here,
Snow - flakes in the air,

hap - pi - ness and
car - ols ev - 'ry -

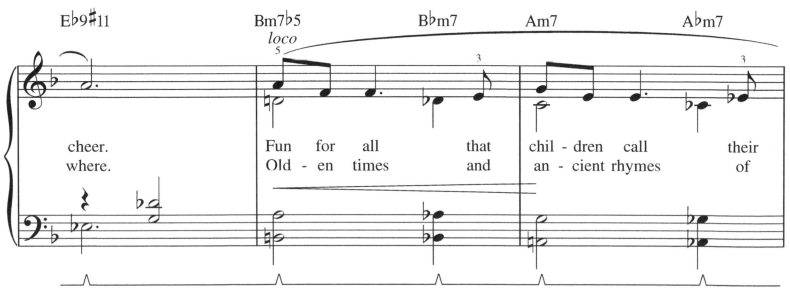

cheer.
where.

Fun for all that
Old - en times and

chil - dren call their
an - cient rhymes their of

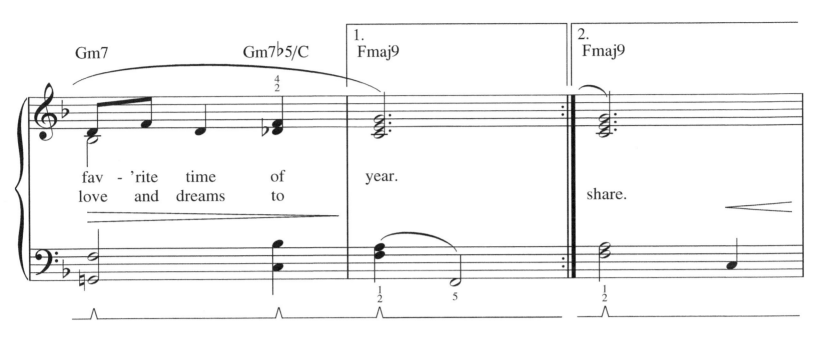

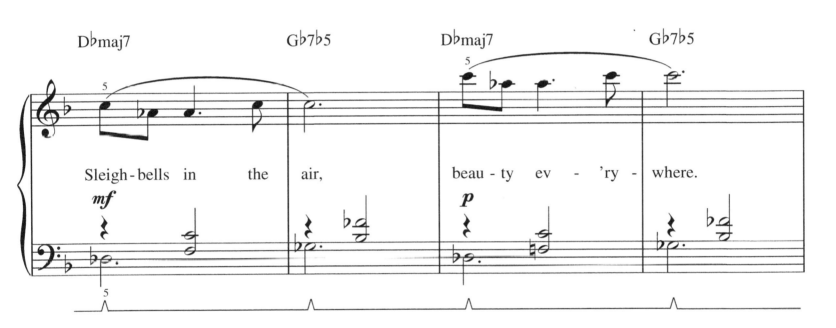

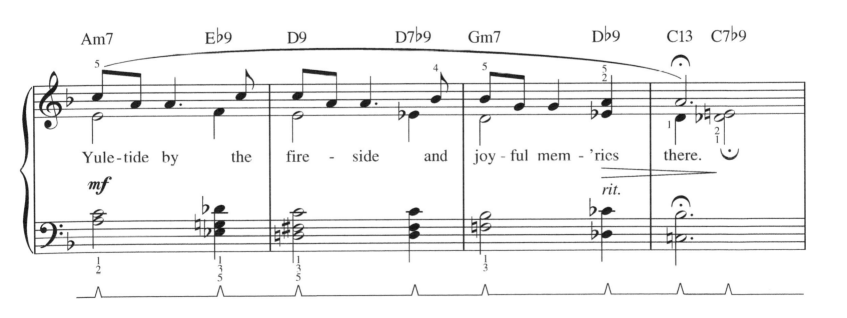

# I'LL BE HOME FOR CHRISTMAS

Words and Music by KIM GANNON
and WALTER KENT
Arranged by Phillip Keveren

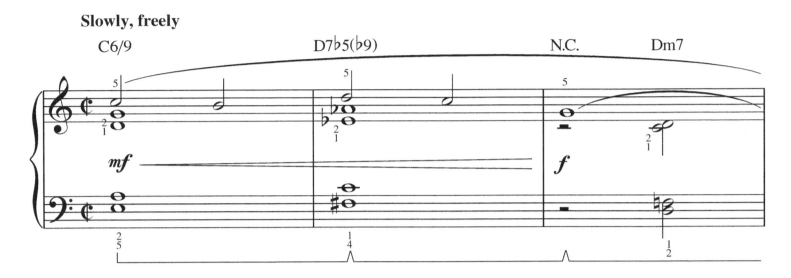

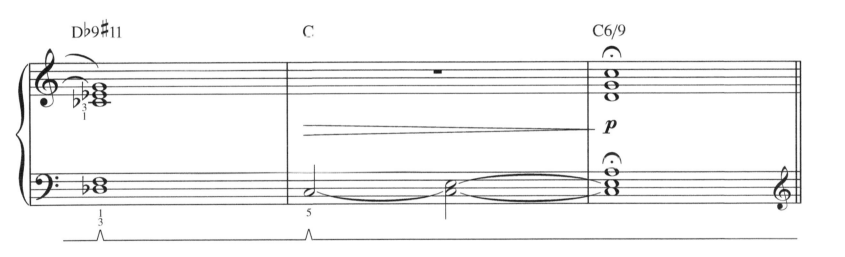

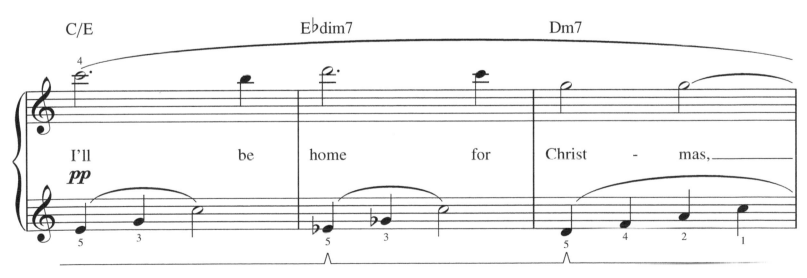

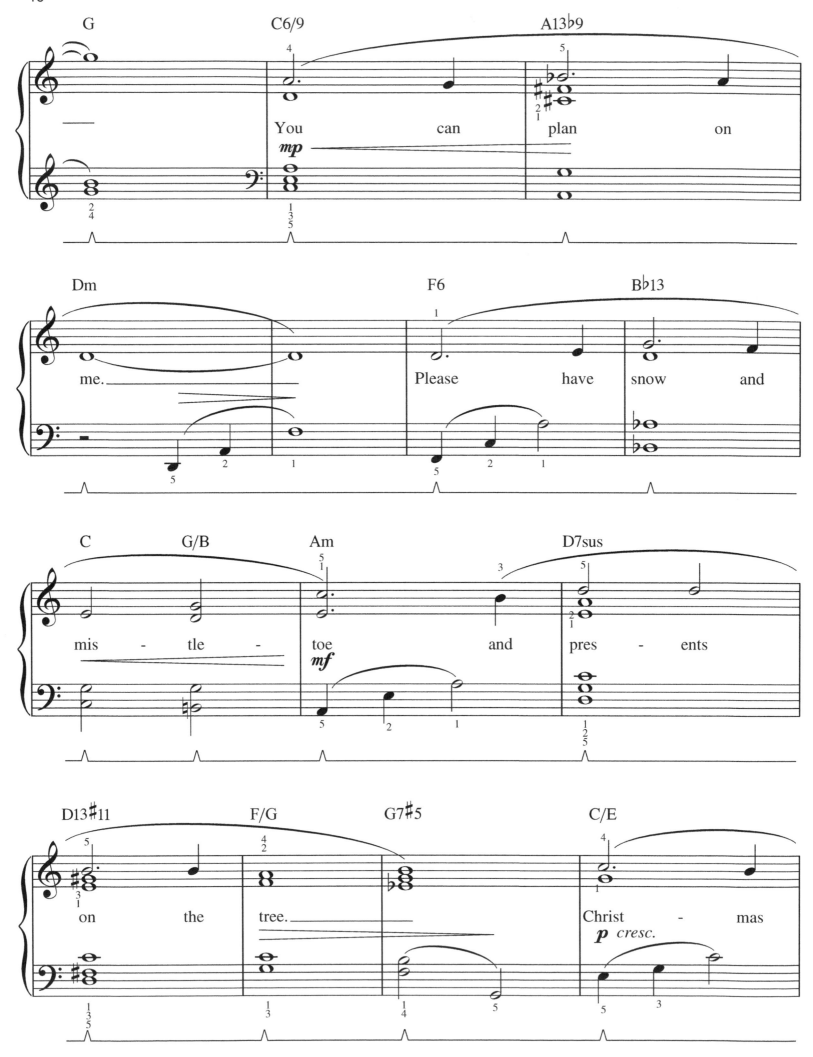

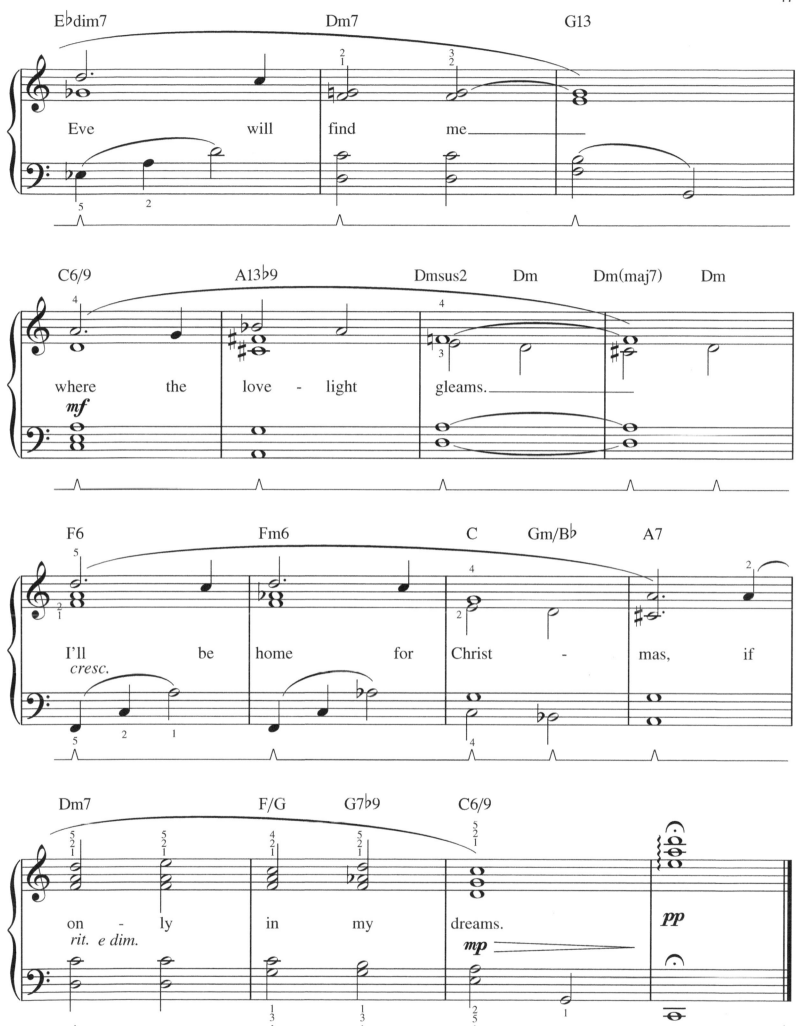

# THE CHRISTMAS WALTZ

Words by SAMMY CAHN
Music by JULE STYNE
Arranged by Phillip Keveren

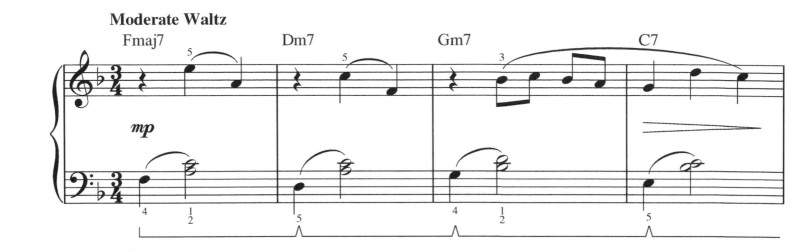

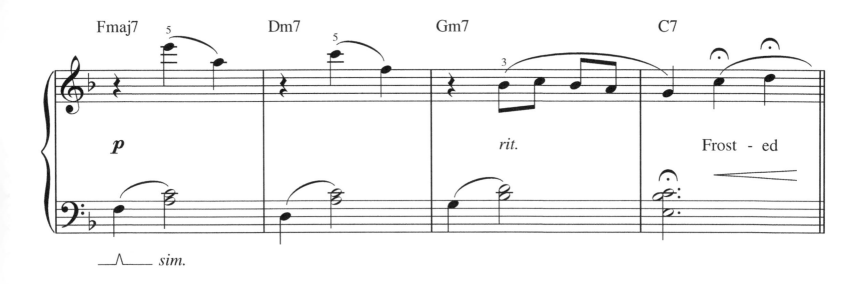

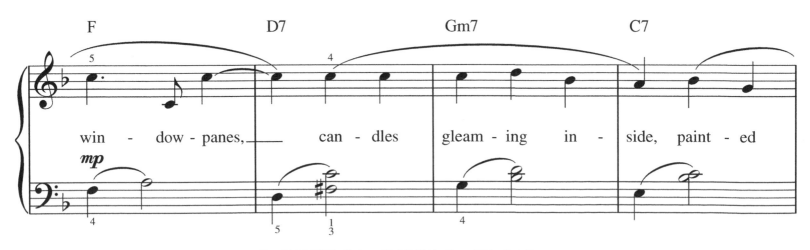

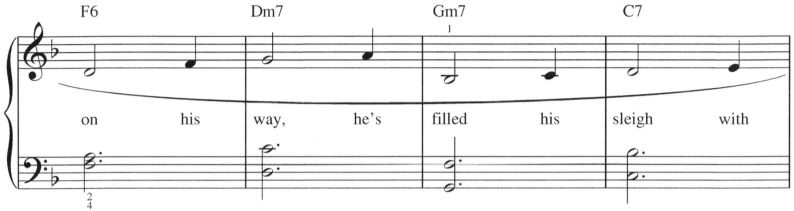

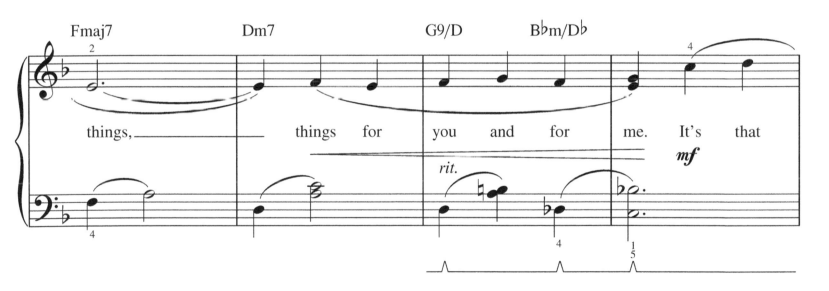

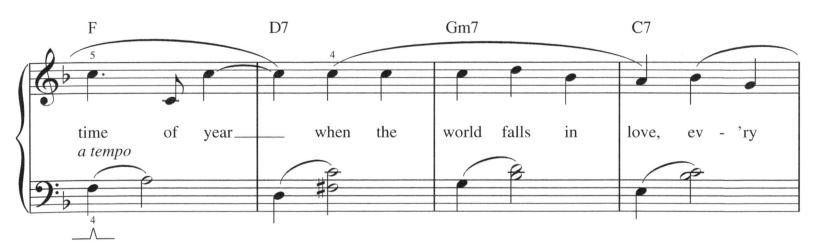

20

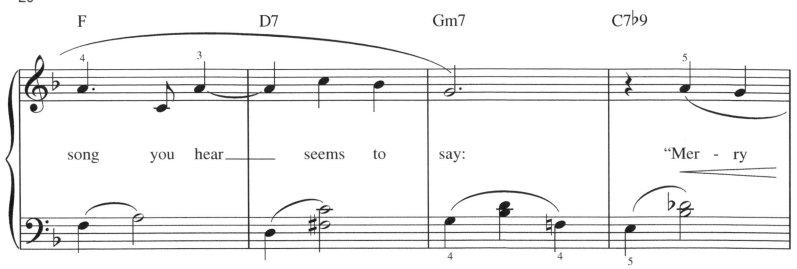

song you hear____ seems to say: "Mer - ry

Christ - mas, May your New Year dreams come

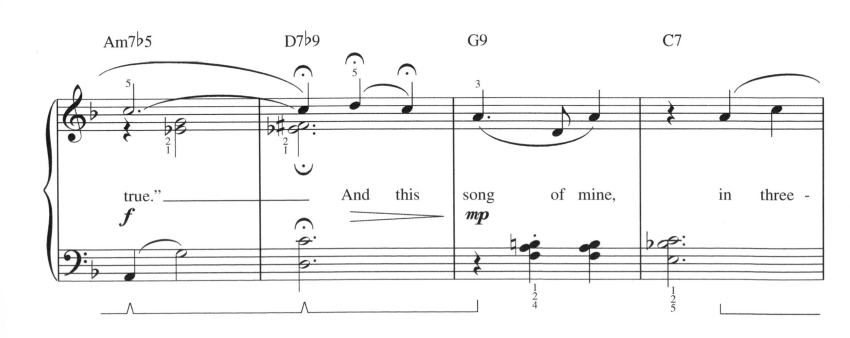

true."____ And this song of mine, in three -

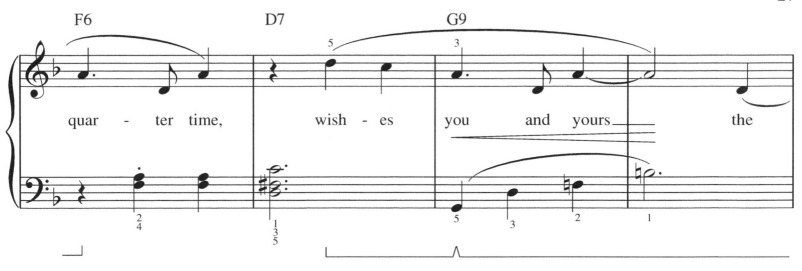

quar - ter time, wish - es you and yours the

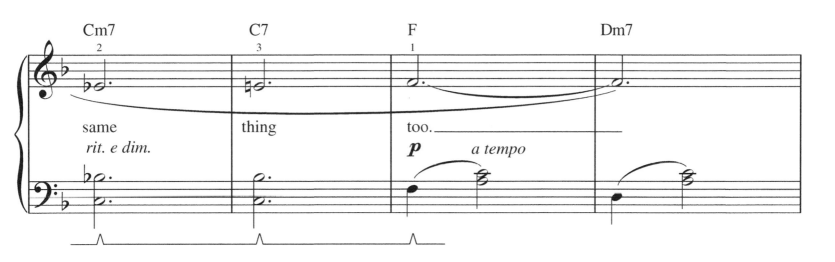

same thing too.
*rit. e dim.* *p* *a tempo*

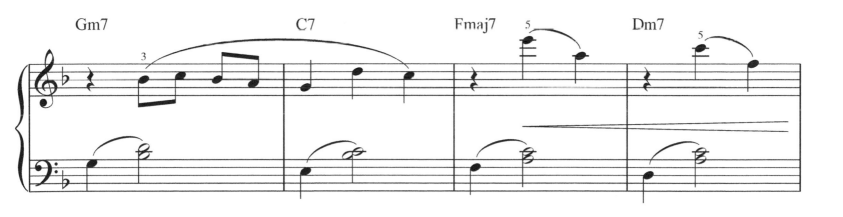

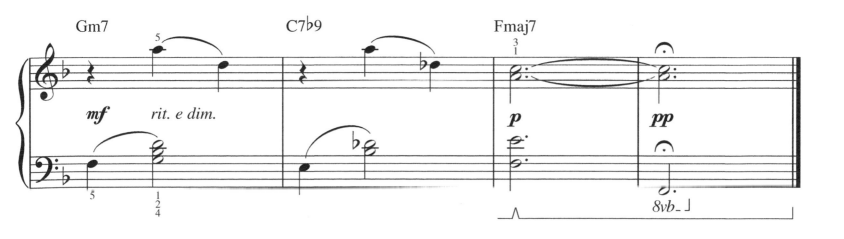

*mf* *rit. e dim.* *p* *pp*

*8vb*

# DO YOU HEAR WHAT I HEAR

Words and Music by NOEL REGNEY
and GLORIA SHAYNE
Arranged by Phillip Keveren

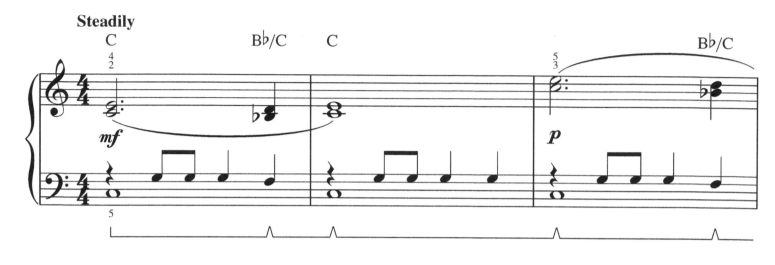

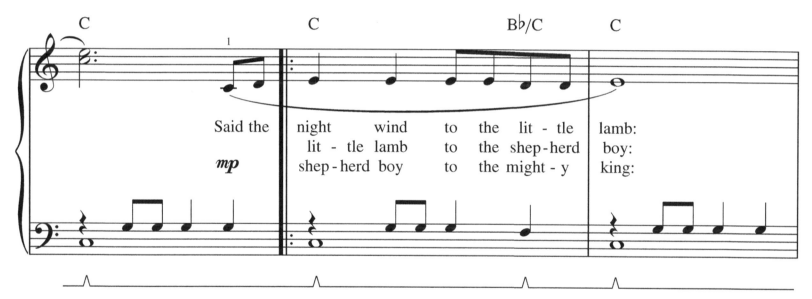

Said the night wind to the lit-tle lamb:
lit-tle lamb to the shep-herd boy:
shep-herd boy to the might-y king:

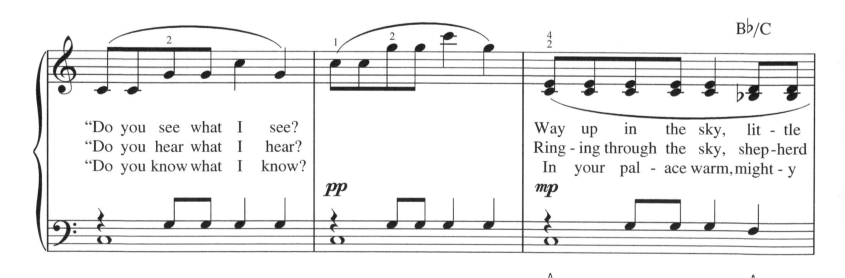

"Do you see what I see?
"Do you hear what I hear?
"Do you know what I know?

Way up in the sky, lit-tle
Ring-ing through the sky, shep-herd
In your pal-ace warm, might-y

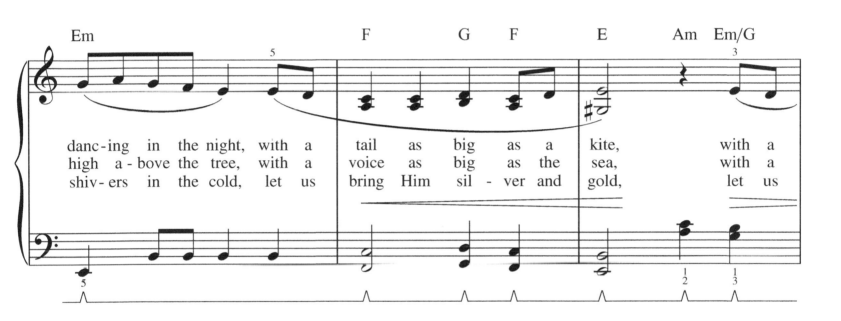

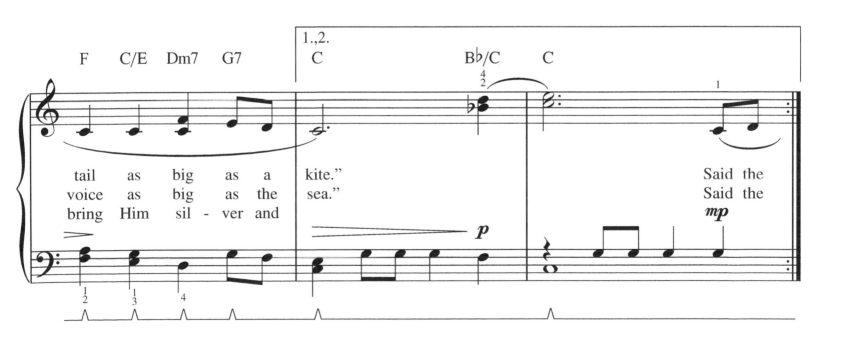

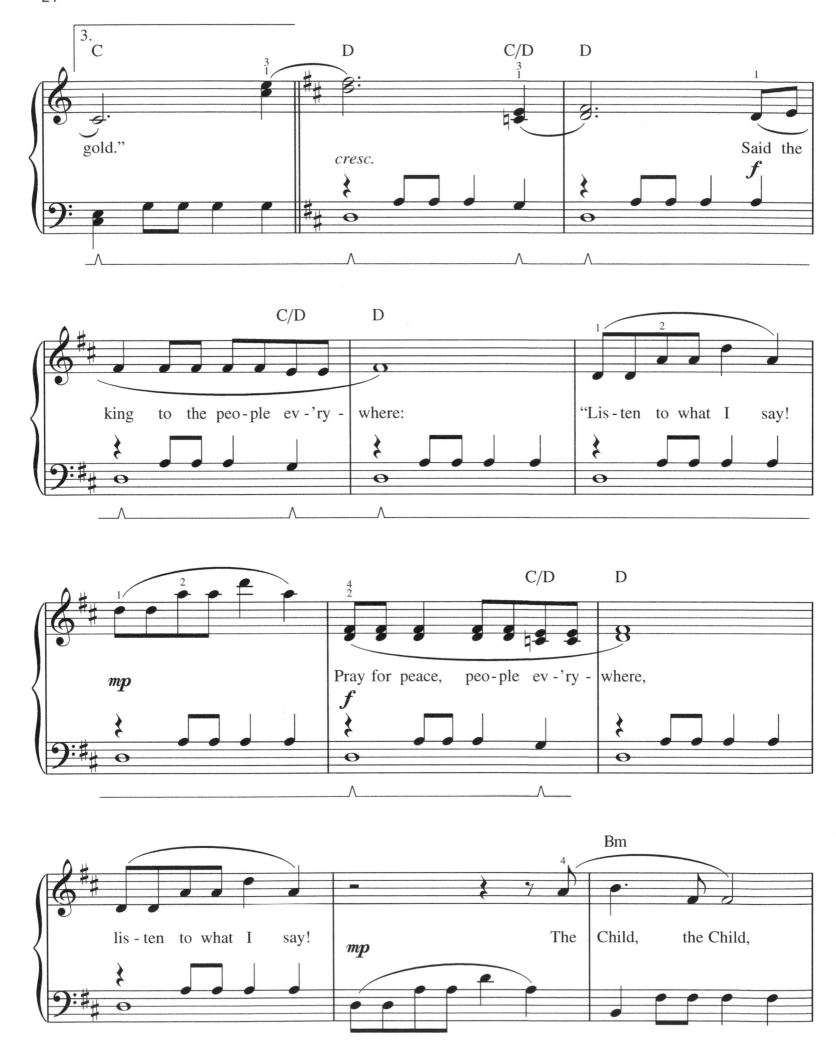

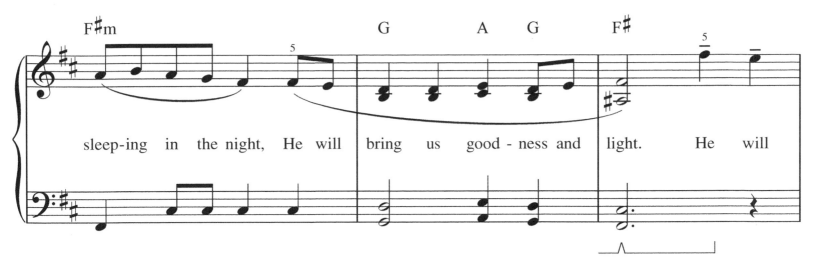

sleep-ing in the night, He will bring us good - ness and light. He will

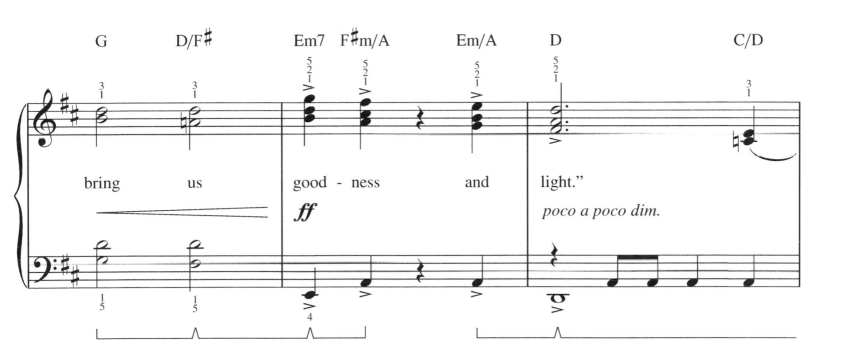

bring us good - ness and light." He will

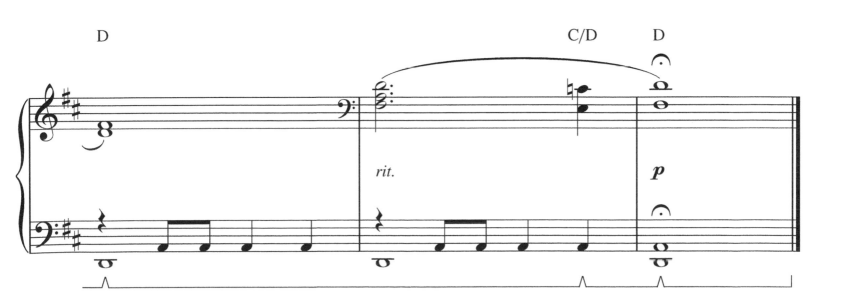

# FROSTY THE SNOW MAN

Words and Music by STEVE NELSON
and JACK ROLLINS
Arranged by Phillip Keveren

**Cheerfully**

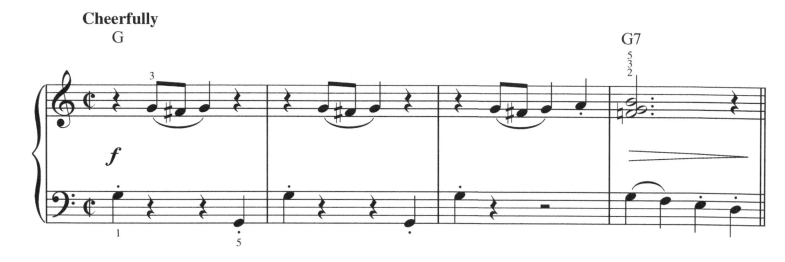

Fros - ty the Snow Man was a jol - ly hap - py
Fros - ty the Snow Man knew the sun was hot that

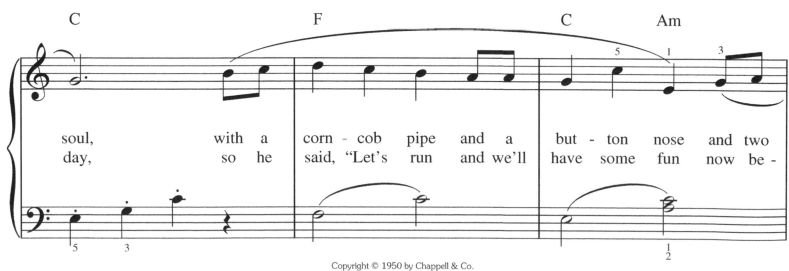

soul, with a corn - cob pipe and a but - ton nose and two
day, so he said, "Let's run and we'll have some fun now be-

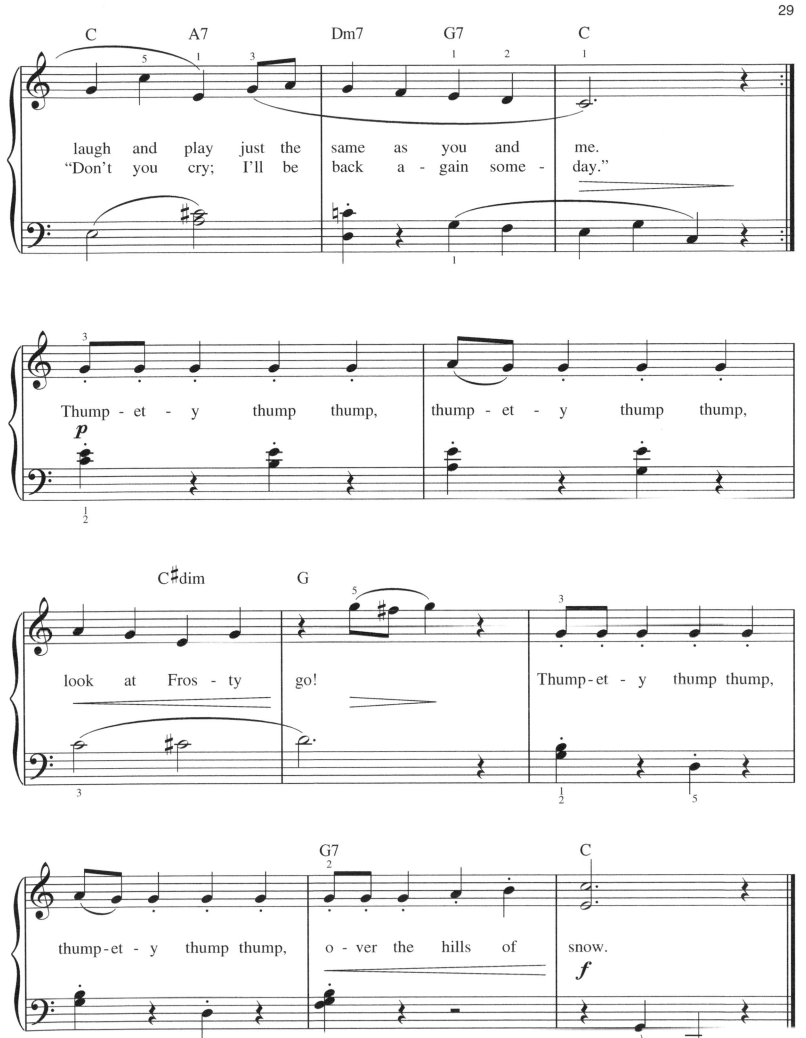

# IT MUST HAVE BEEN THE MISTLETOE

### (Our First Christmas)

By JUSTIN WILDE
and DOUG KONECKY
Arranged by Phillip Keveren

**Moderately**

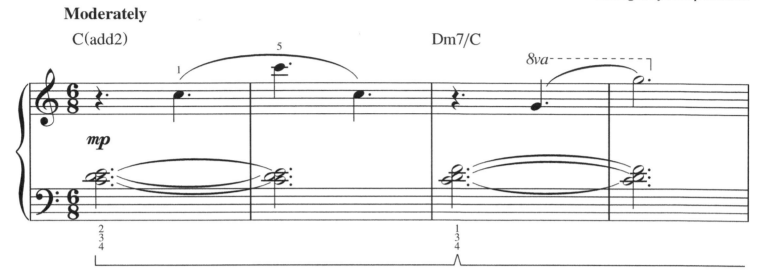

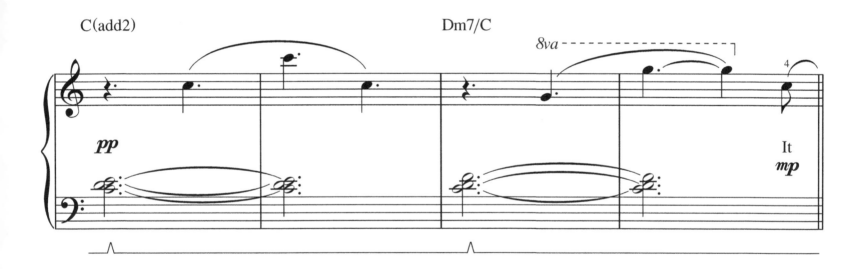

must have been___ the mis - tle - toe,___ the la - zy fire,___ the

___ sim.

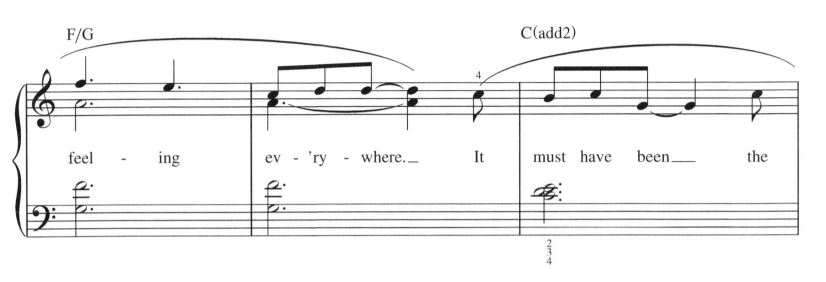

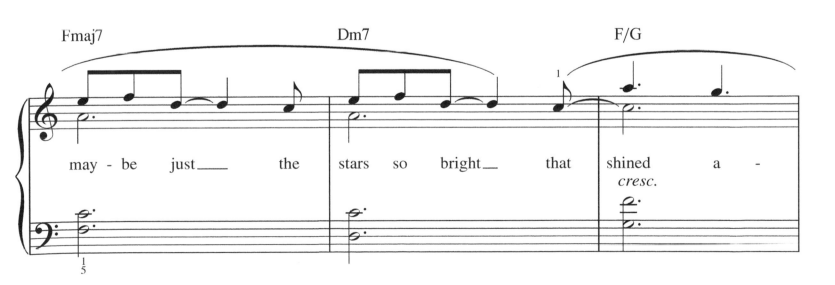

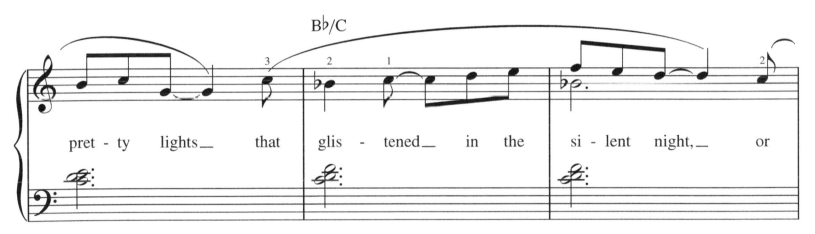

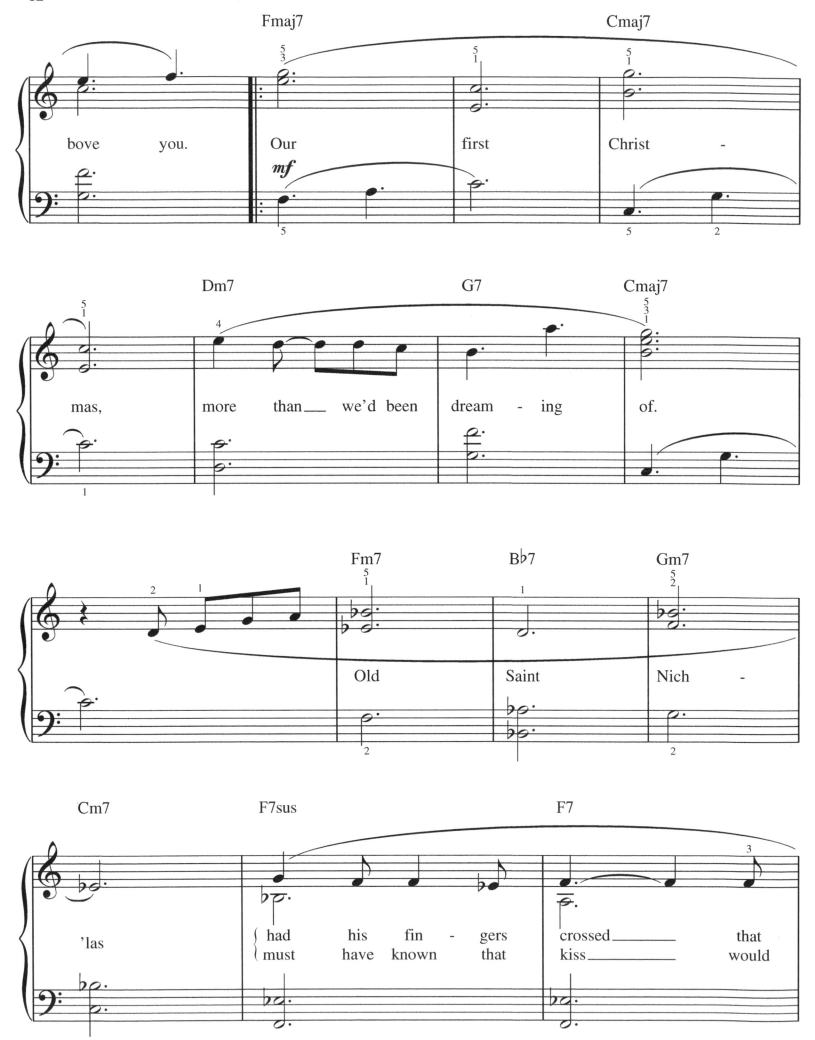

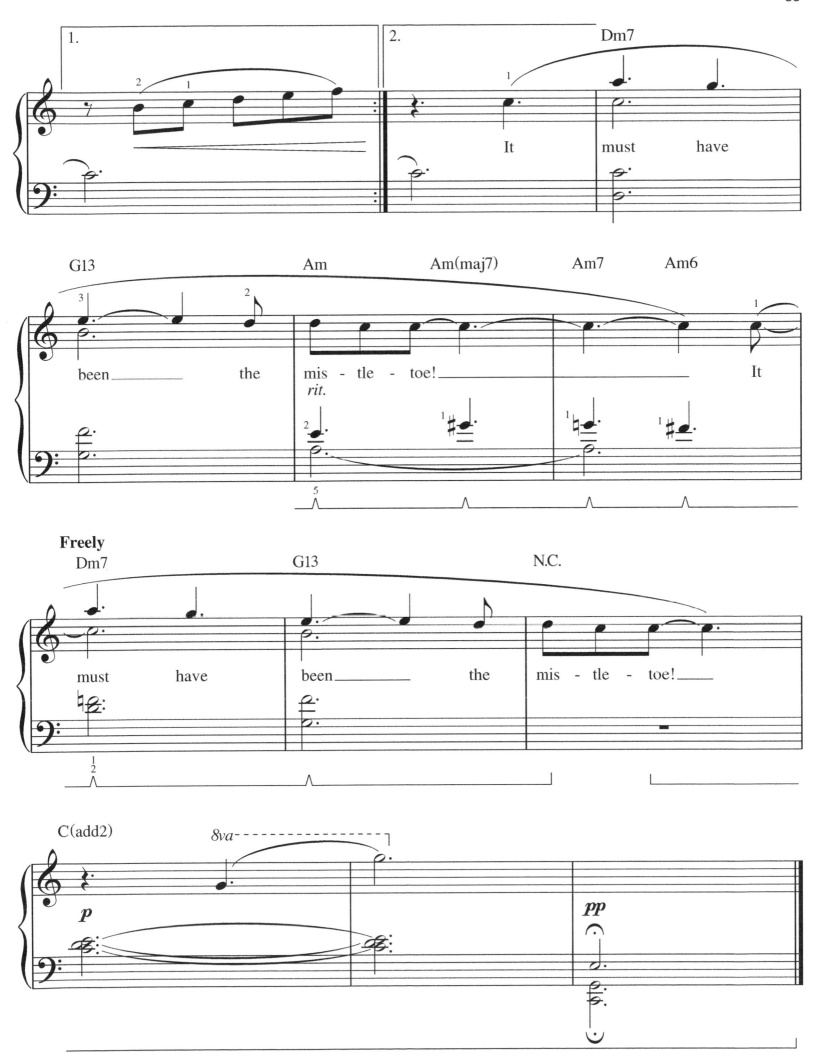

# MARY, DID YOU KNOW?

Words and Music by MARK LOWRY
and BUDDY GREENE
Arranged by Phillip Keveren

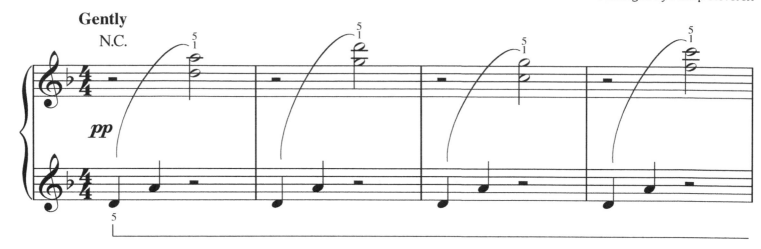

Mar - y, did you | know      that your
              know      that your
              know      that your

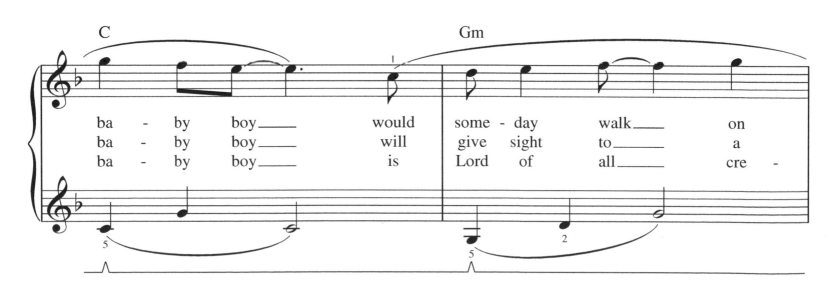

ba - by boy____ would | some - day walk____ on
ba - by boy____ will | give sight to____ a
ba - by boy____ is | Lord of all____ cre -

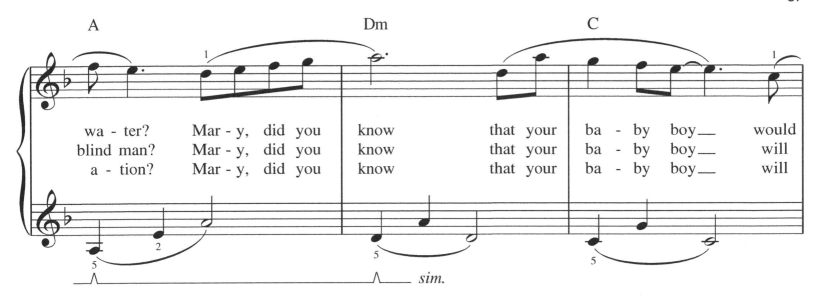

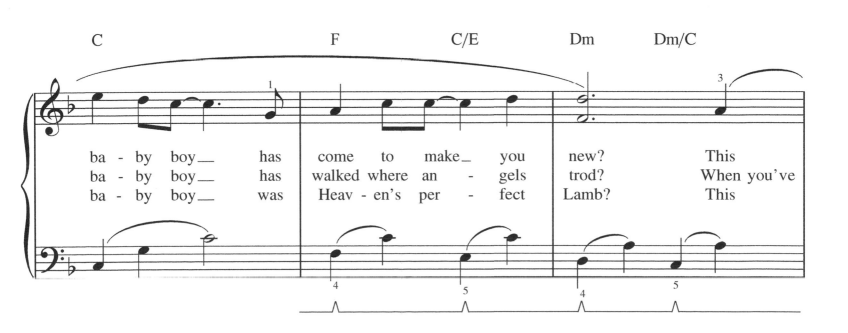

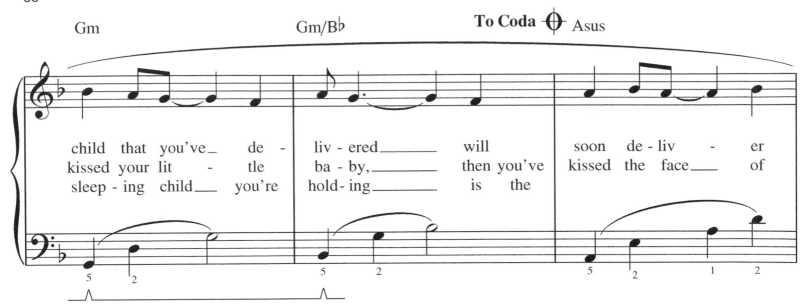

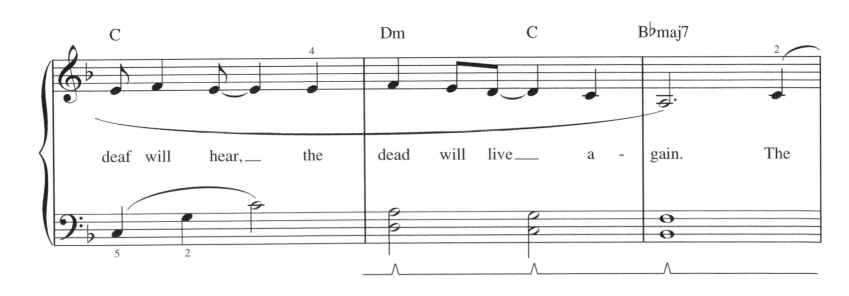

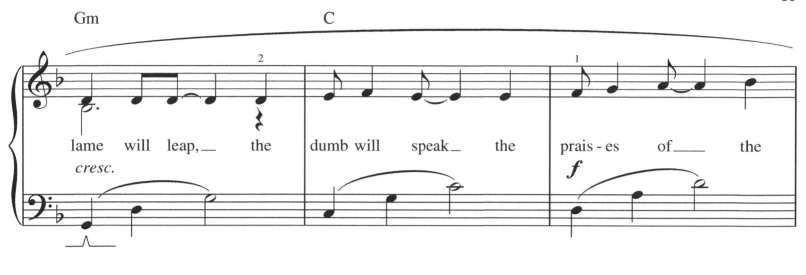

lame will leap,___ the dumb will speak___ the prais-es of___ the

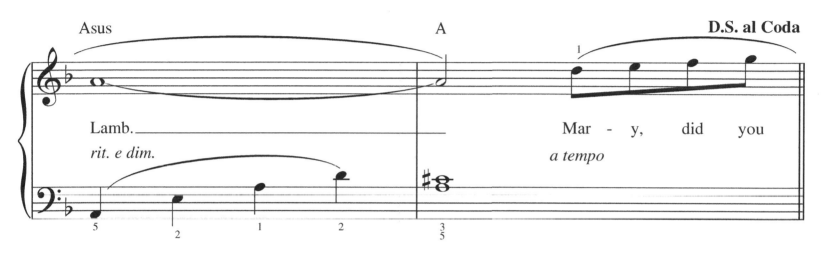

Lamb.___ Mar - y, did you

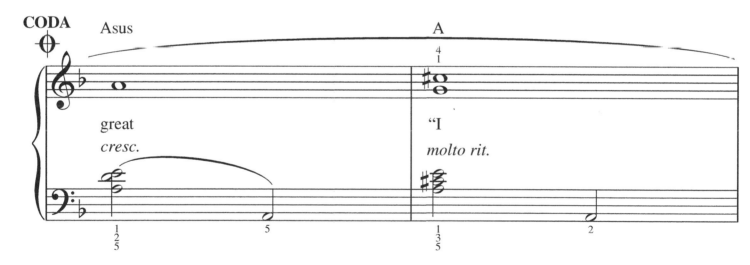

great "I

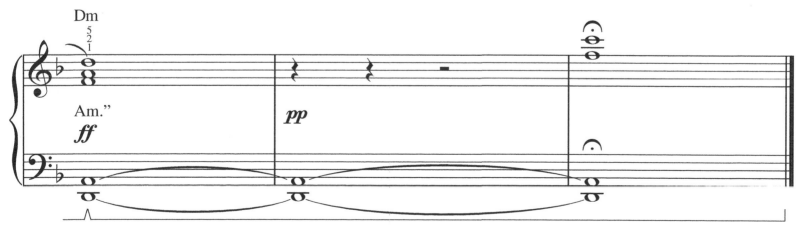

Am." pp

# MERRY CHRISTMAS, DARLING

Words and Music by RICHARD CARPENTER
and FRANK POOLER
Arranged by Phillip Keveren

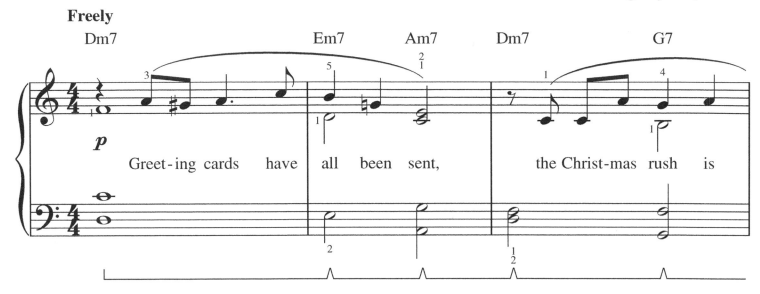

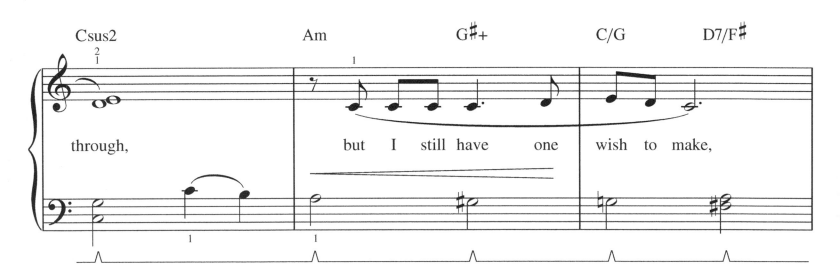

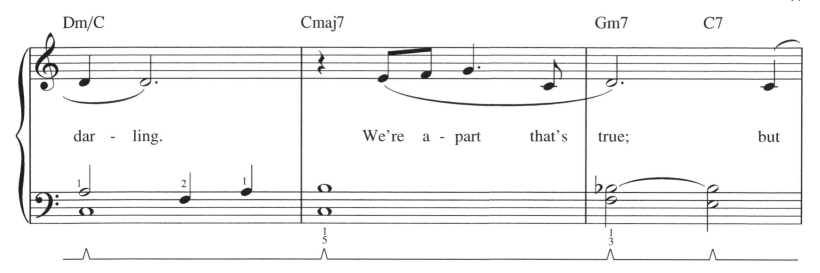

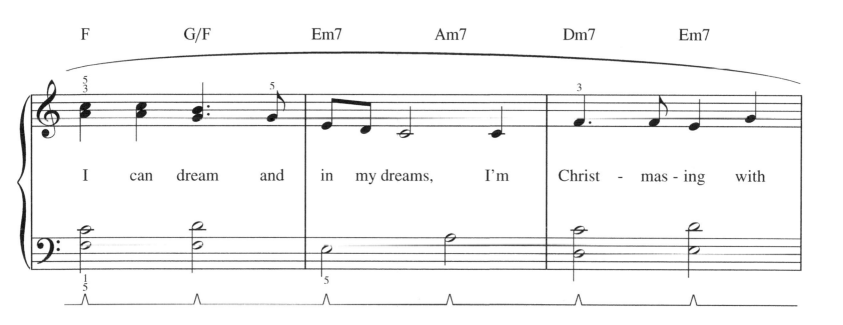

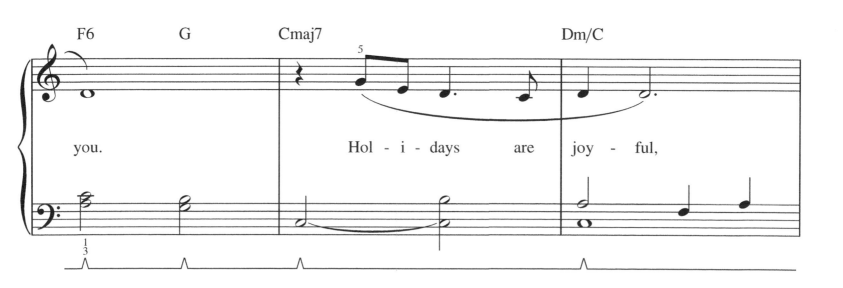

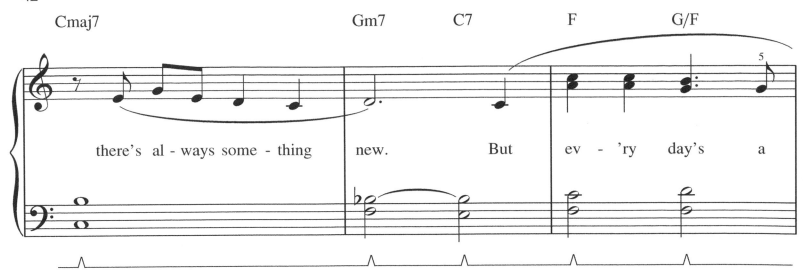

there's al - ways some - thing new. But ev - 'ry day's a

hol - i - day when I'm near to you. The

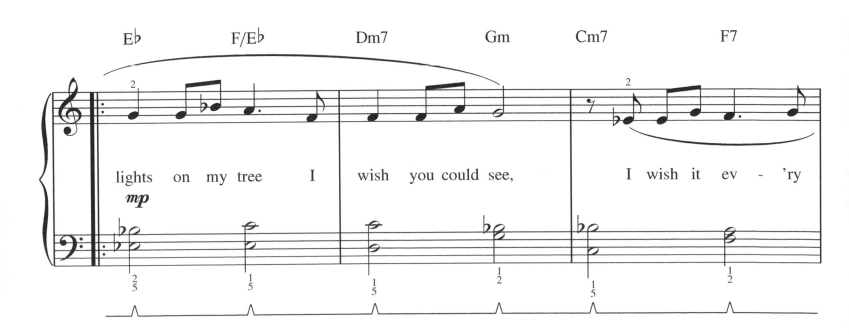

lights on my tree I wish you could see, I wish it ev - 'ry

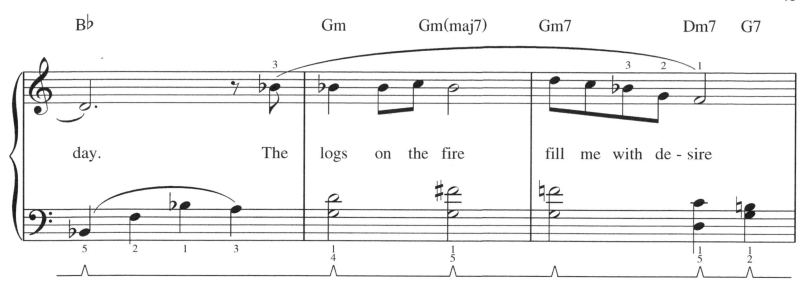

day.  The  logs  on  the  fire  fill  me  with  de - sire

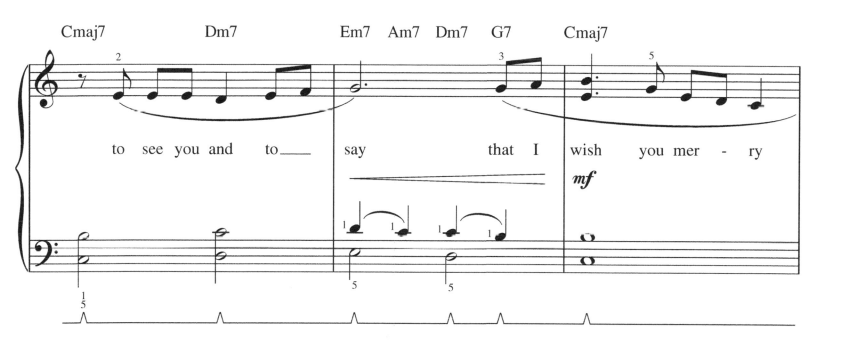

to  see  you  and  to____  say  that  I  wish  you  mer - ry

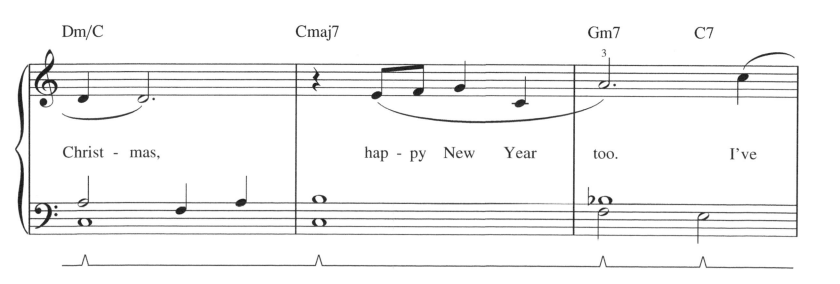

Christ - mas,  hap - py  New  Year  too.  I've

44

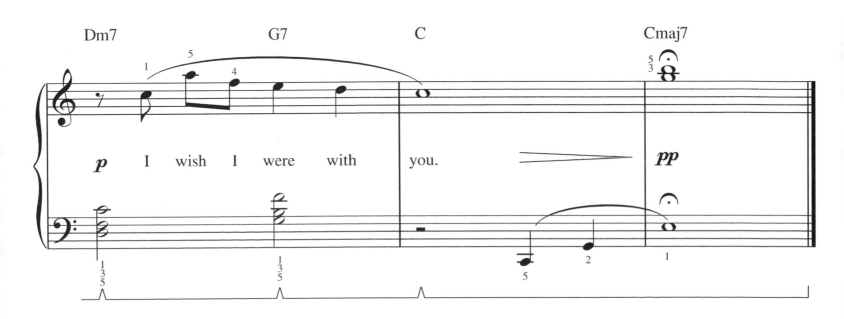

# THE MOST WONDERFUL TIME OF THE YEAR

Words and Music by EDDIE POLA
and GEORGE WYLE
Arranged by Phillip Keveren

**Bright Waltz**

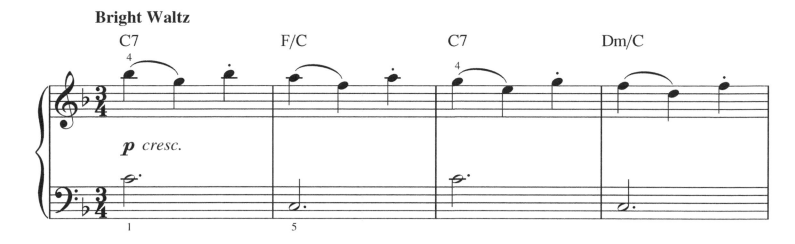

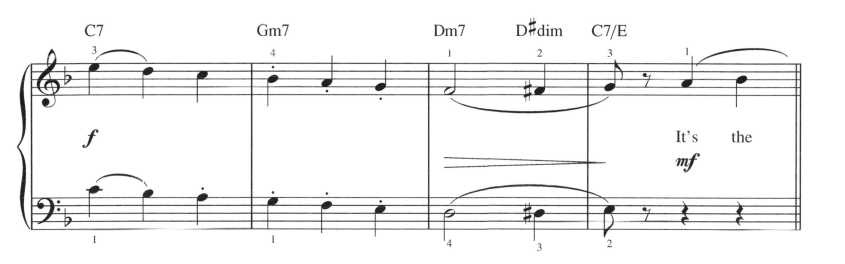

It's the

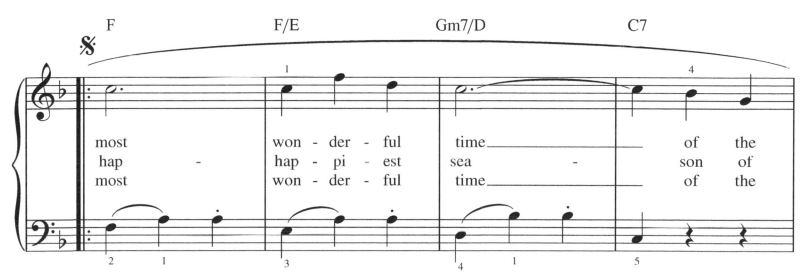

most ... won-der-ful time ... of the
hap - hap-pi - est sea - son of
most won-der-ful time ... of the

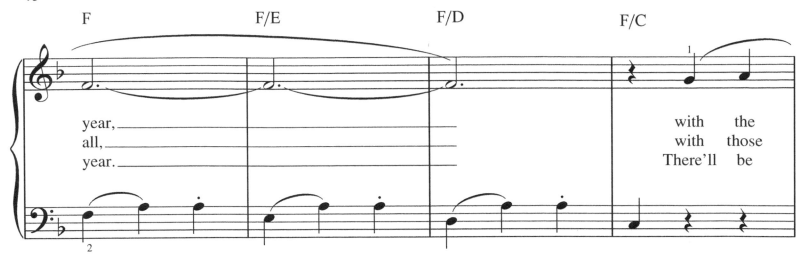

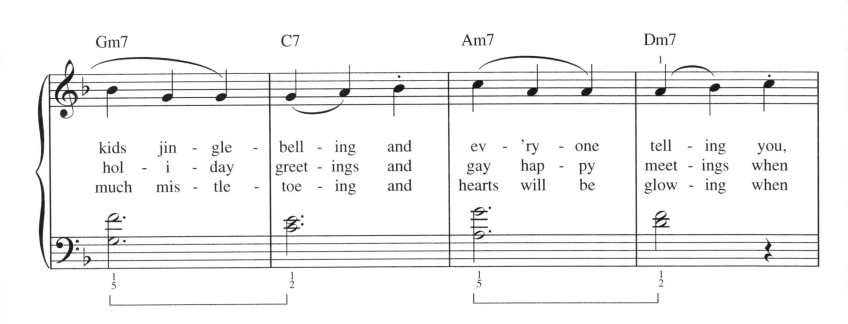

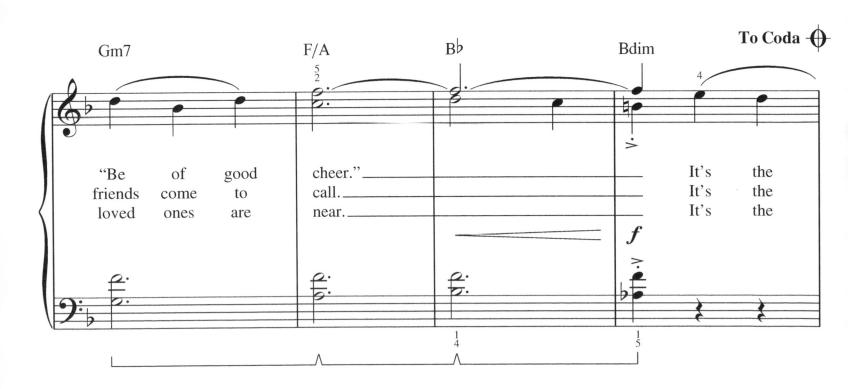

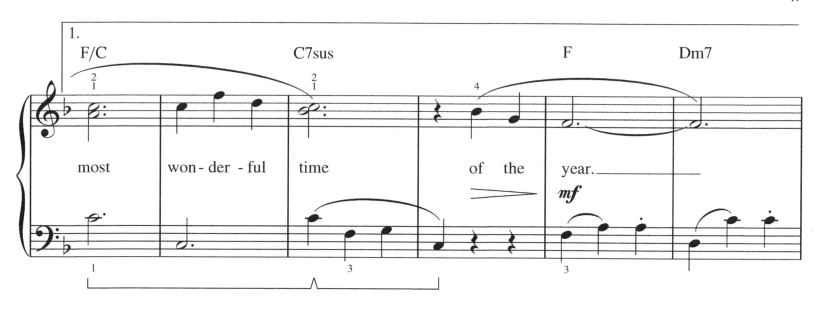

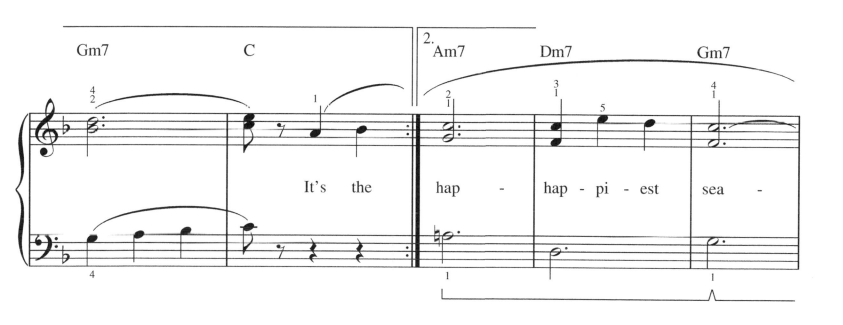

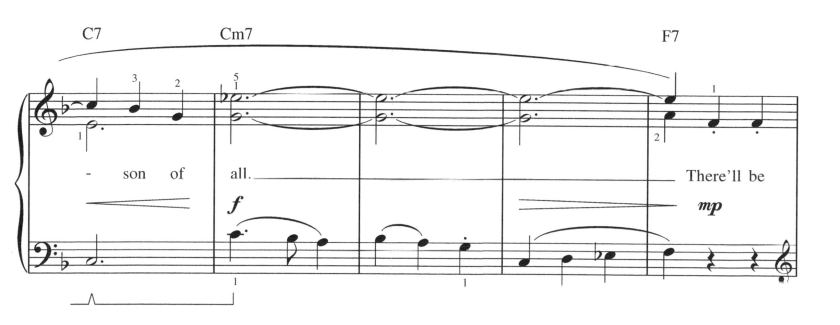

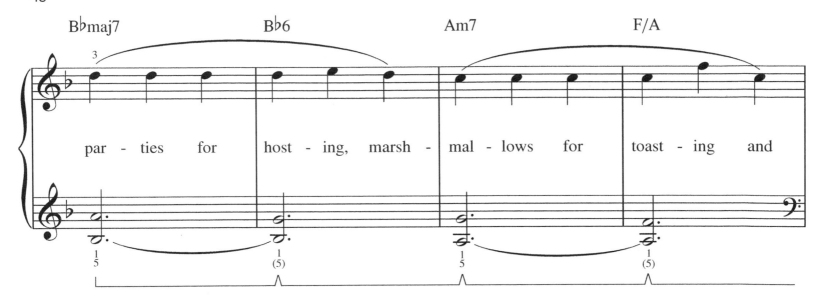

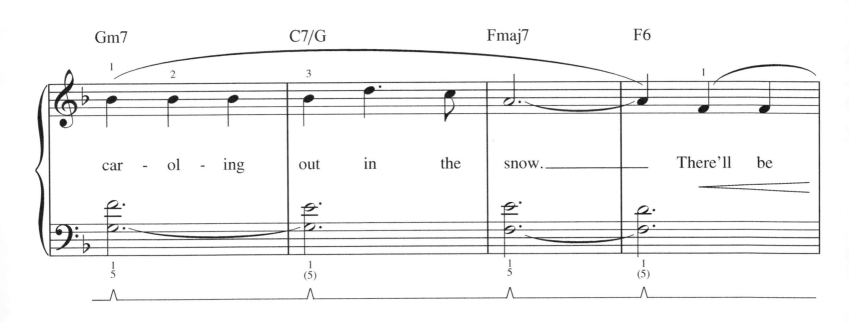

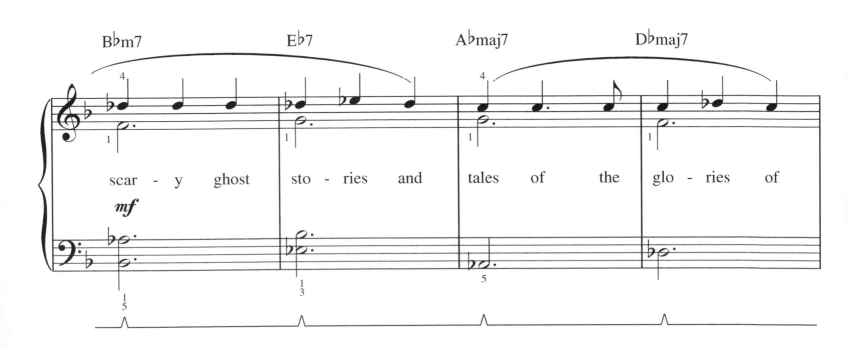

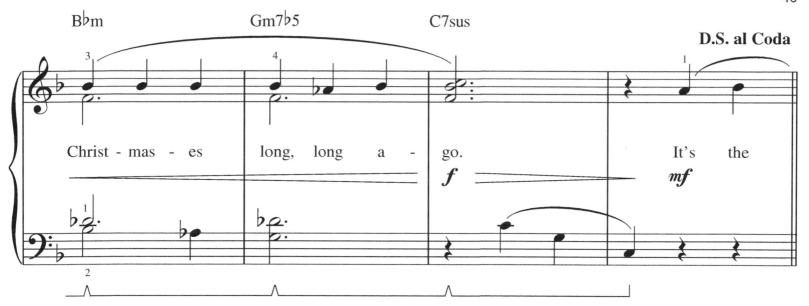

**D.S. al Coda**

Christ - mas - es     long, long a - go.     It's the

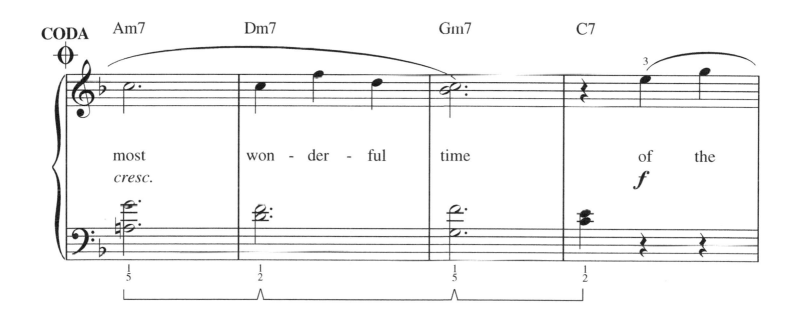

**CODA**

most     won - der - ful     time     of the

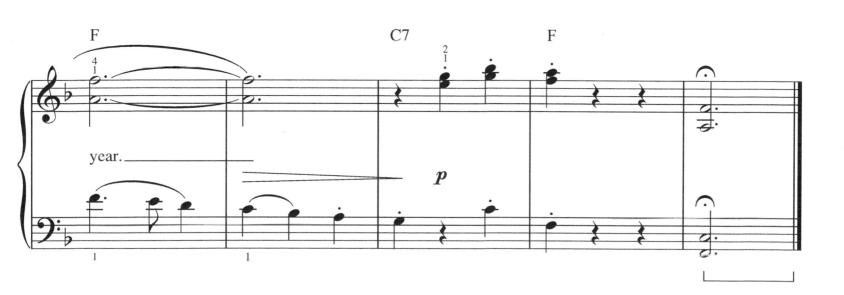

year.

# MIRACLES

By KENNY G
and WALTER AFANASIEFF
Arranged by Phillip Keveren

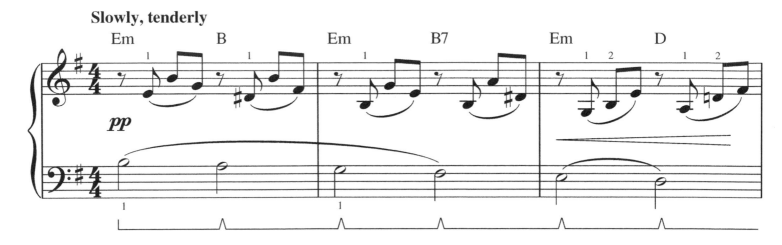

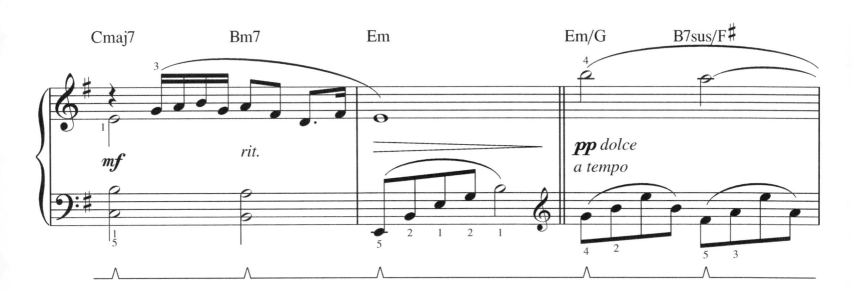

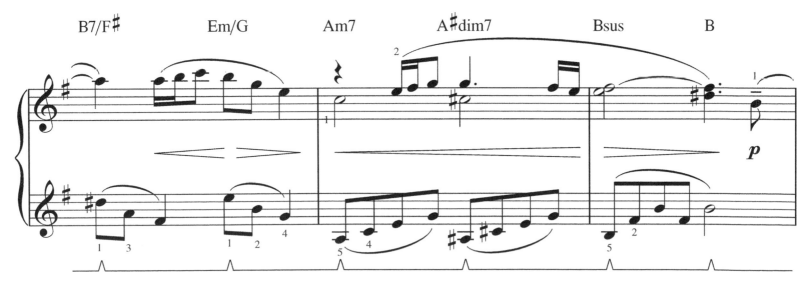

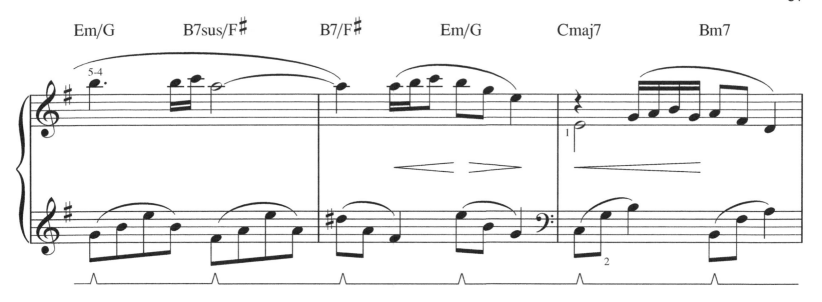

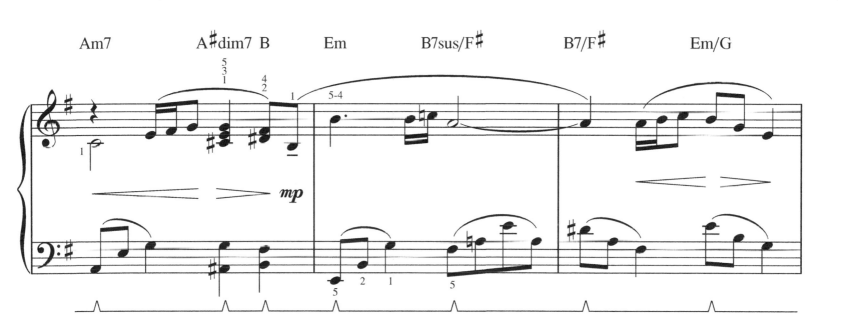

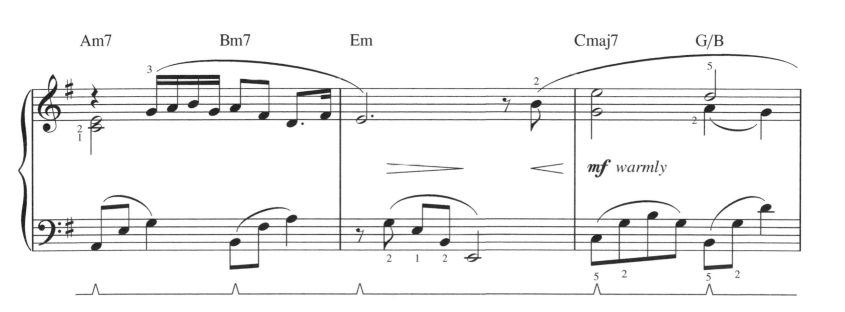

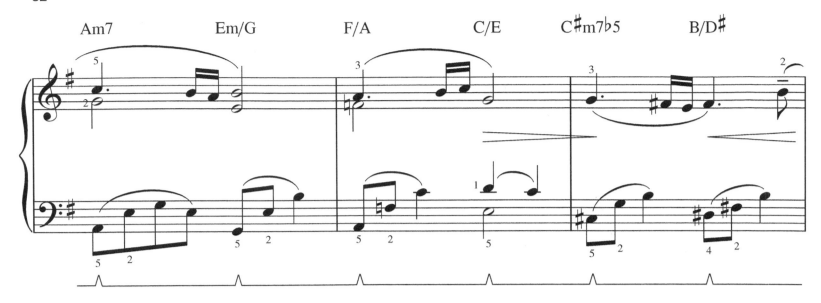

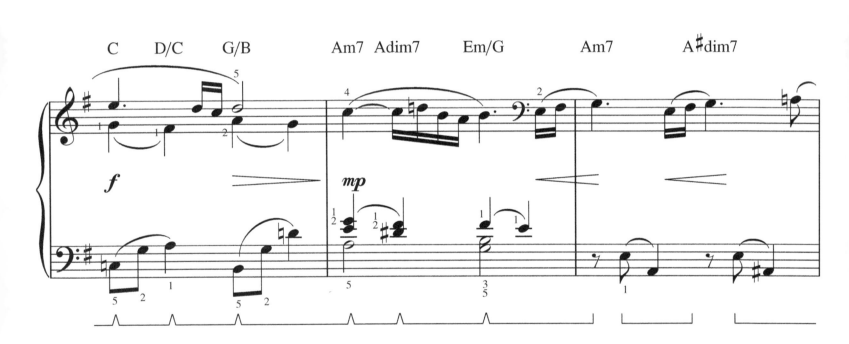

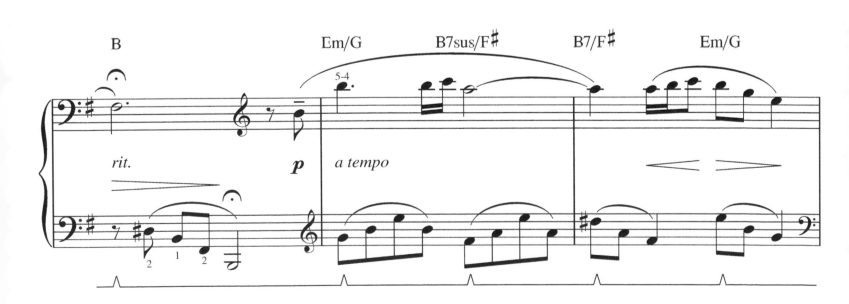

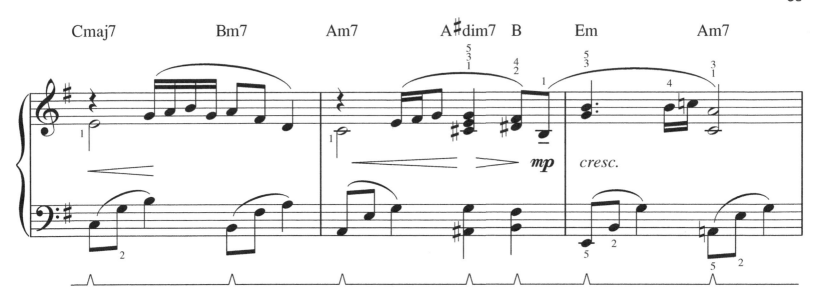

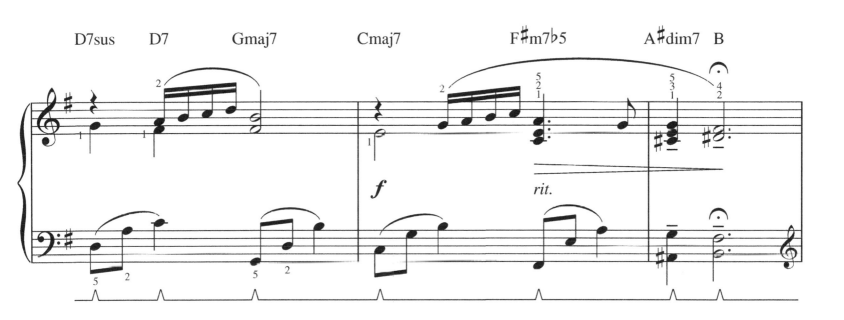

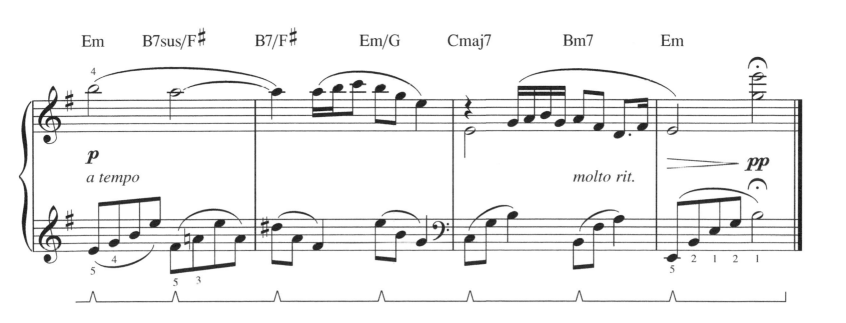

# ROCKIN' AROUND THE CHRISTMAS TREE

Music and Lyrics by JOHNNY MARKS
Arranged by Phillip Keveren

**Moderate Rock**

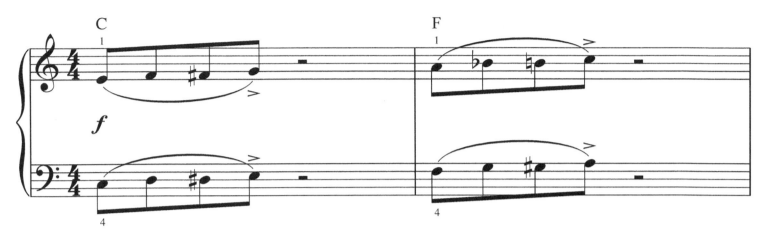

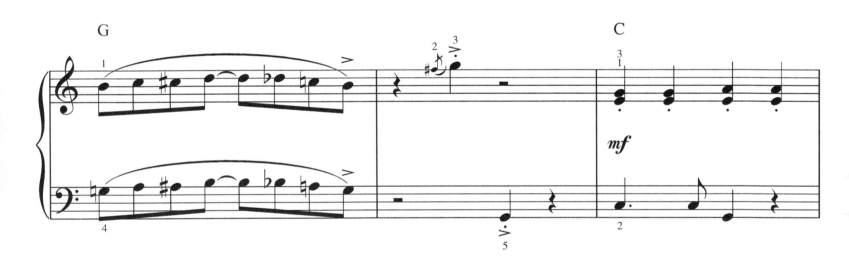

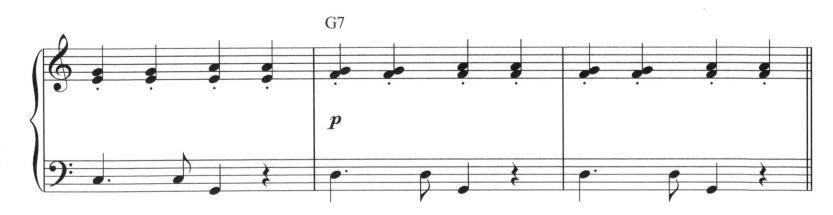

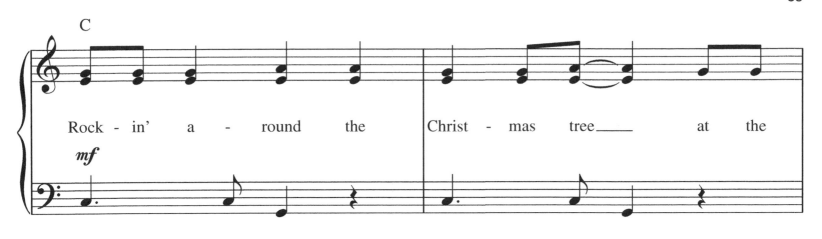

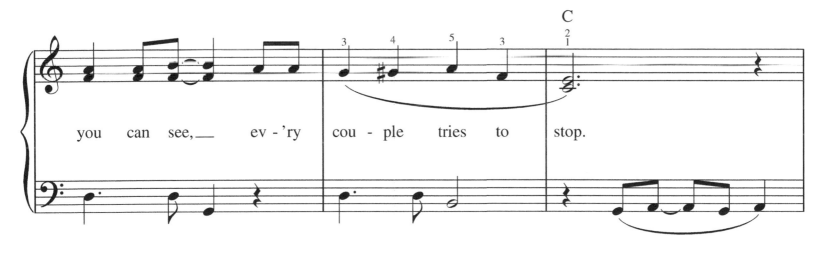

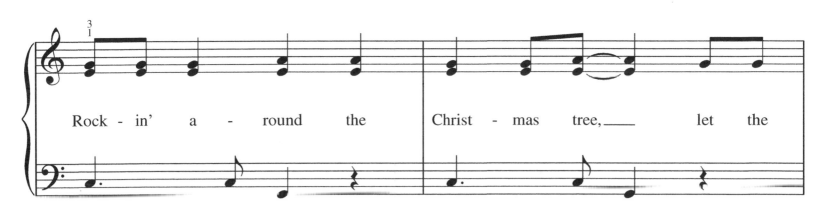

# RUDOLPH, THE RED-NOSED REINDEER

Music and Lyrics by JOHNNY MARKS
Arranged by Phillip Keveren

**Slowly, freely**

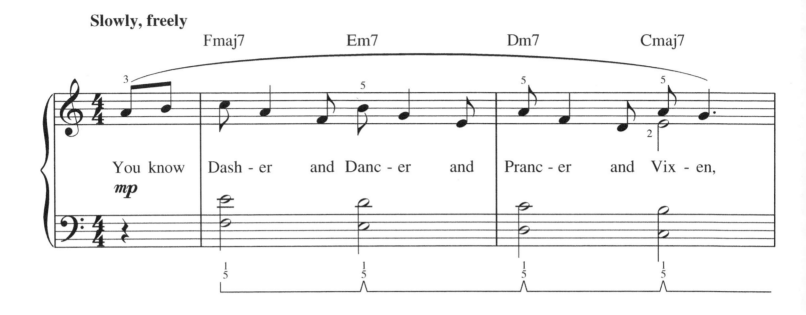

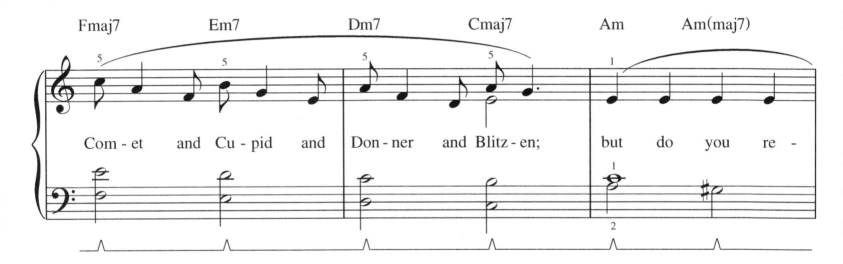

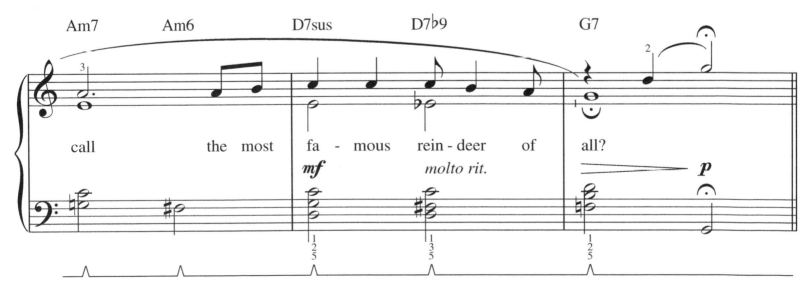

# TENNESSEE CHRISTMAS

Words and Music by AMY GRANT
and GARY CHAPMAN
Arranged by Phillip Keveren

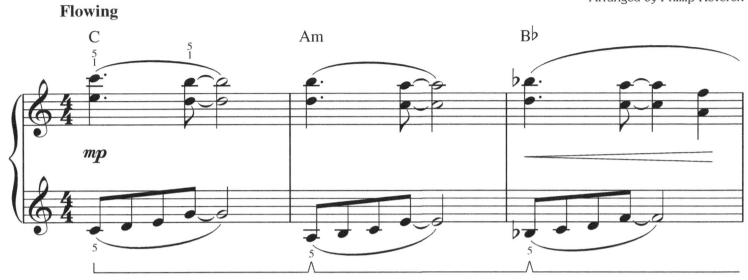

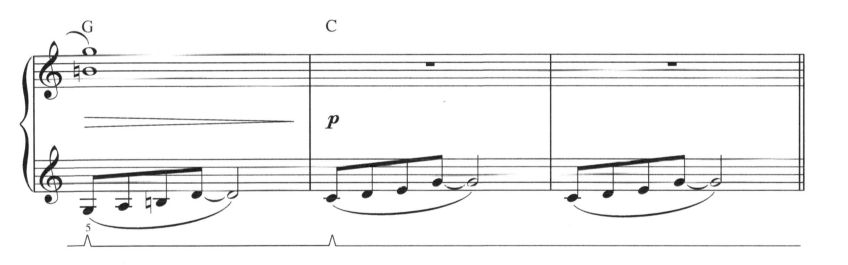

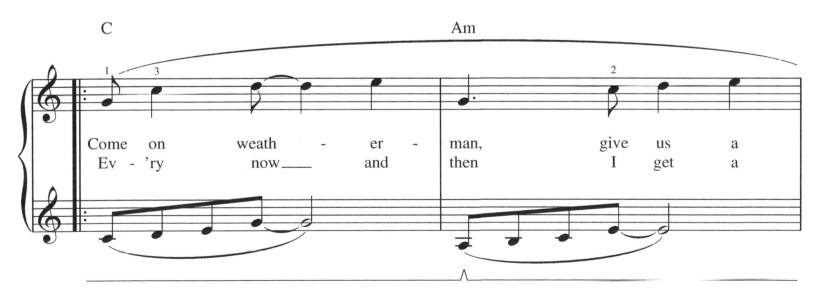

Come on weath - er - man, give us a
Ev - 'ry now ___ and then I get a

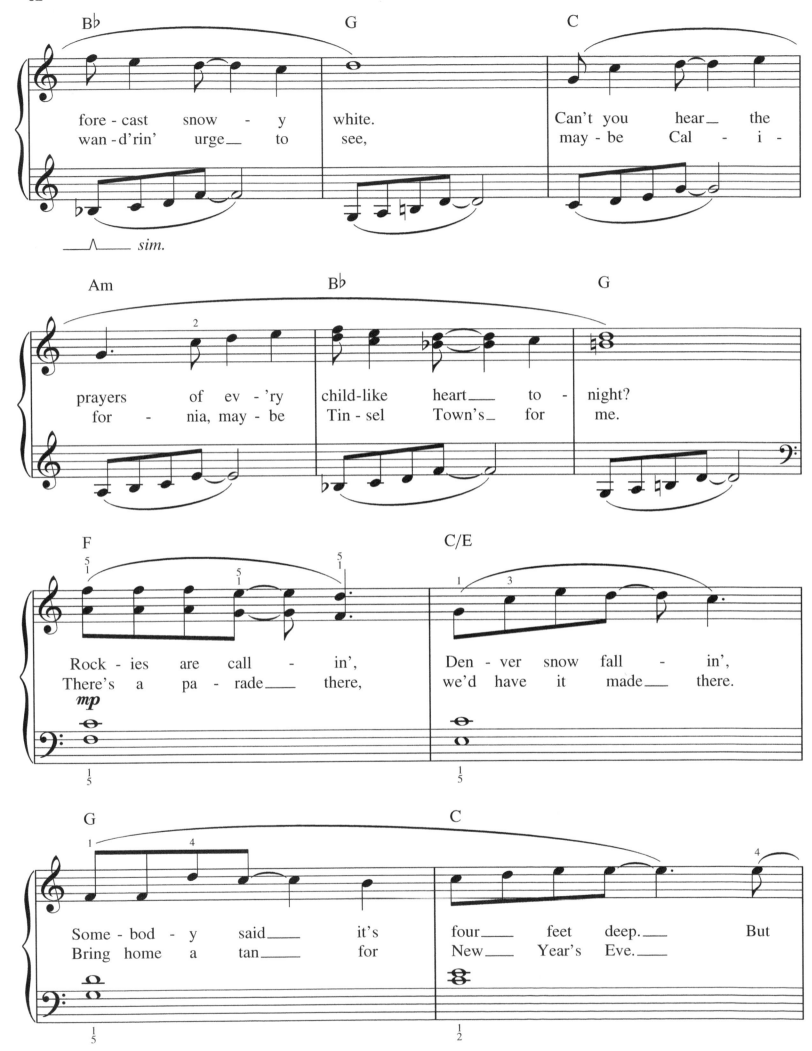

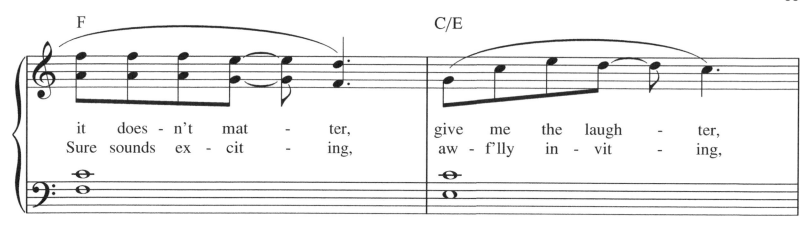

it does - n't mat - ter,   give me the laugh - ter,
Sure sounds ex - cit - ing,   aw - f'lly in - vit - ing,

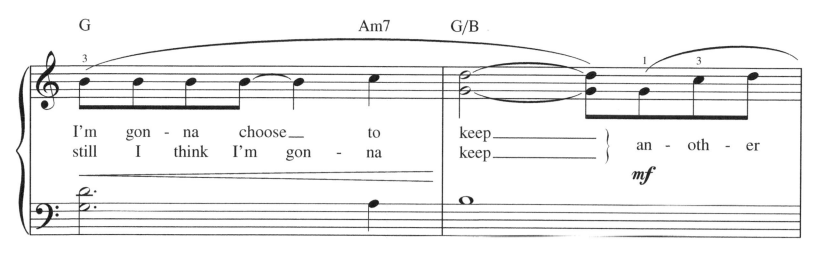

I'm gon - na choose___ to   keep_____   an - oth - er
still I think I'm gon - na   keep_____

mf

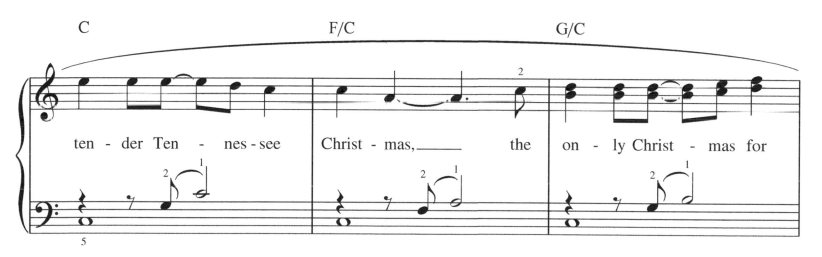

ten - der Ten - nes - see   Christ - mas,_____ the   on - ly Christ - mas for

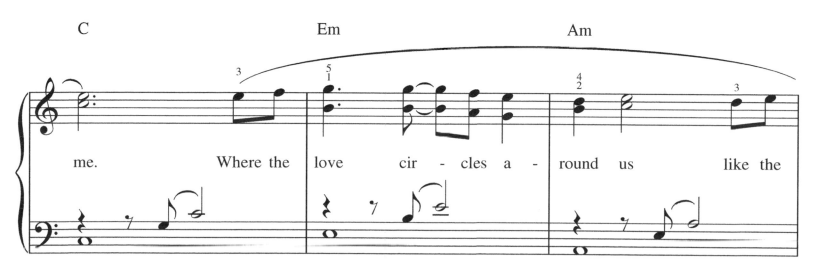

me.   Where the love cir - cles a - round us   like the

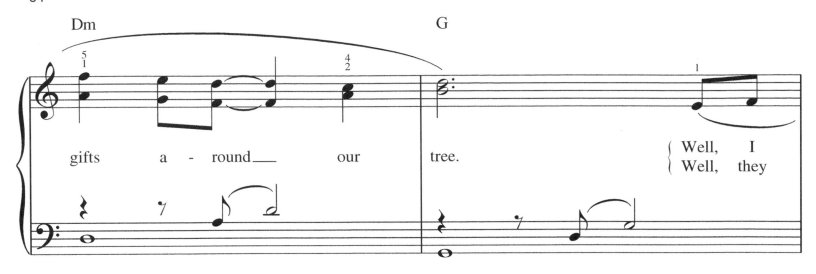

gifts a - round___ our tree.

Well, I
Well, they

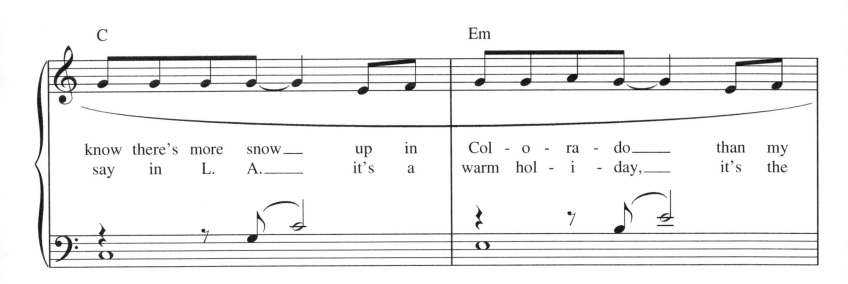

know there's more snow___ up in Col - o - ra - do___ than my
say in L. A.___ it's a warm hol - i - day,___ it's the

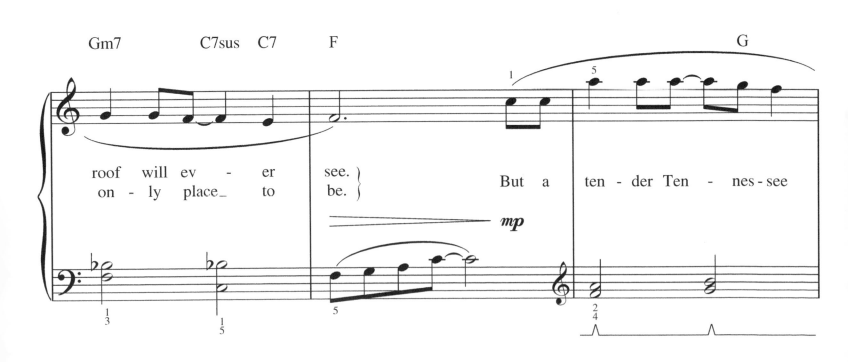

roof will ev - er see.
on - ly place_ to be.

But a ten - der Ten - nes - see

*mp*

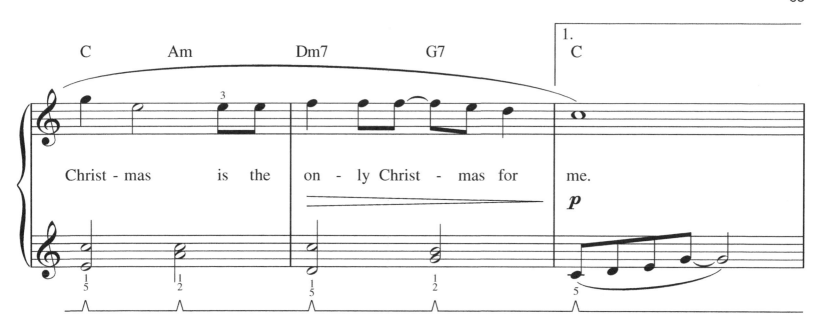

Christ - mas is the on - ly Christ - mas for me.

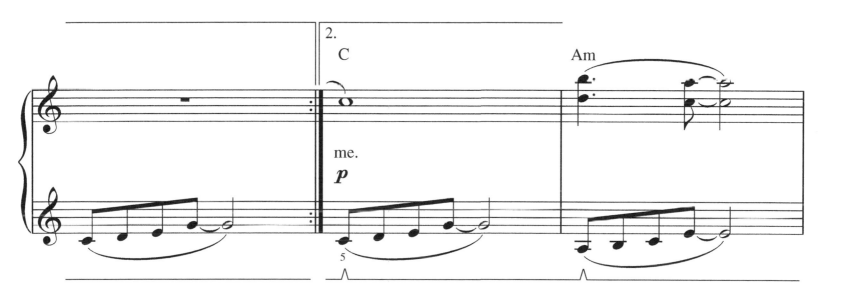

me.

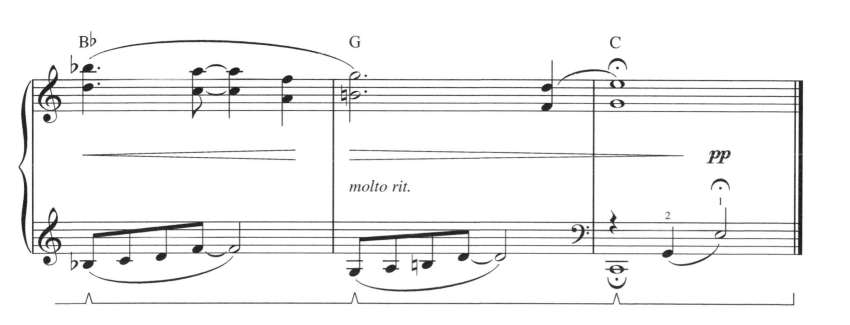

molto rit.

# SILVER BELLS
## from the Paramount Picture THE LEMON DROP KID

Words and Music by JAY LIVINGSTON
and RAY EVANS
Arranged by Phillip Keveren

**Moderate Waltz**

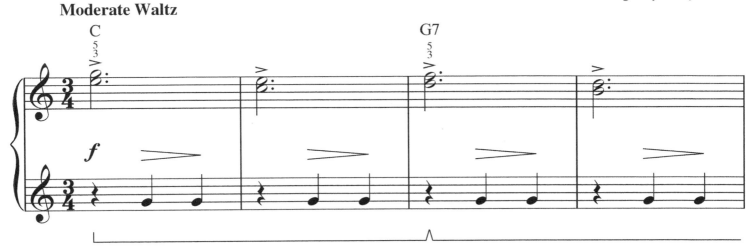

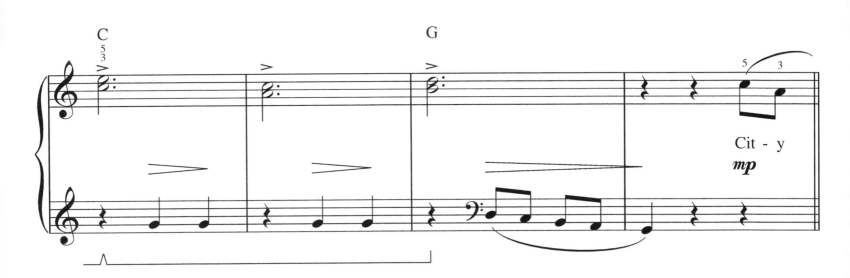

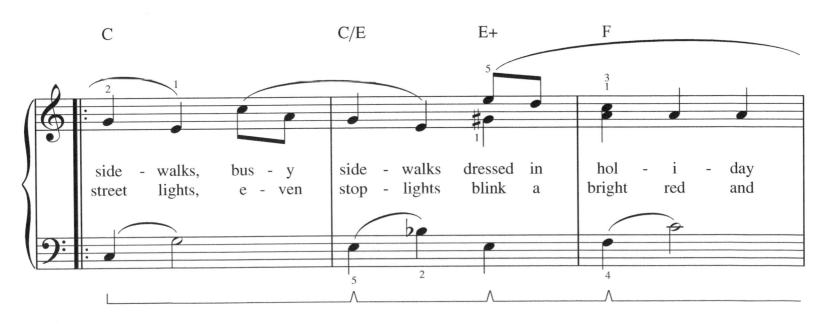

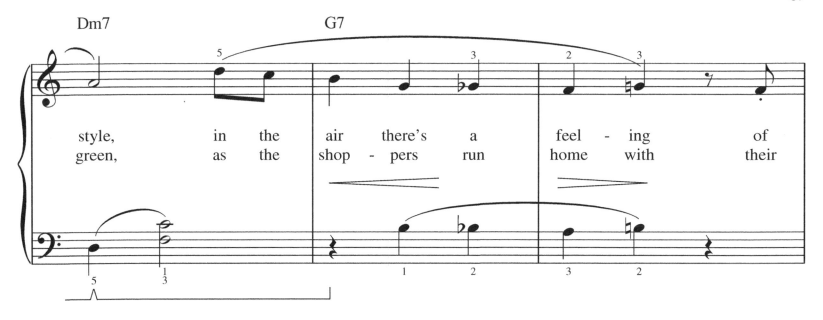

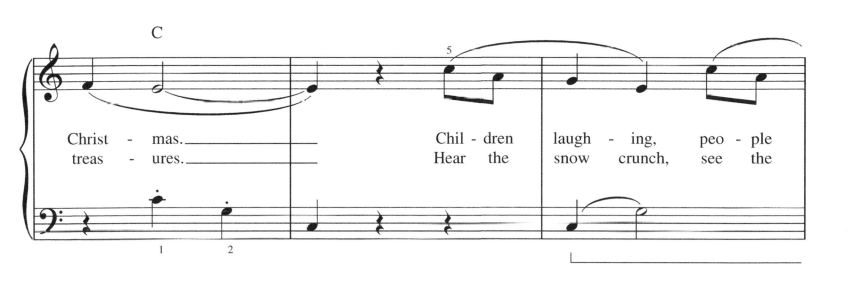

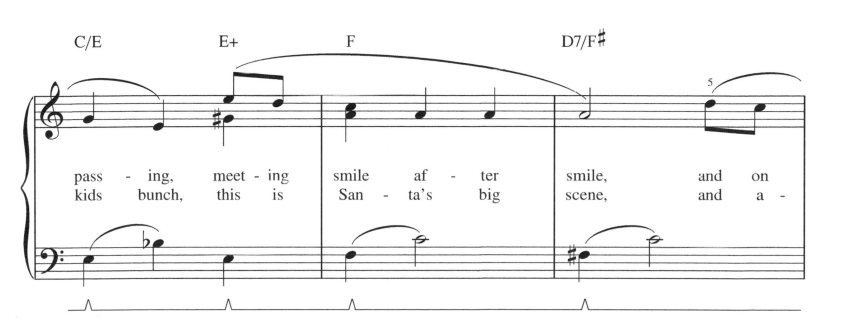

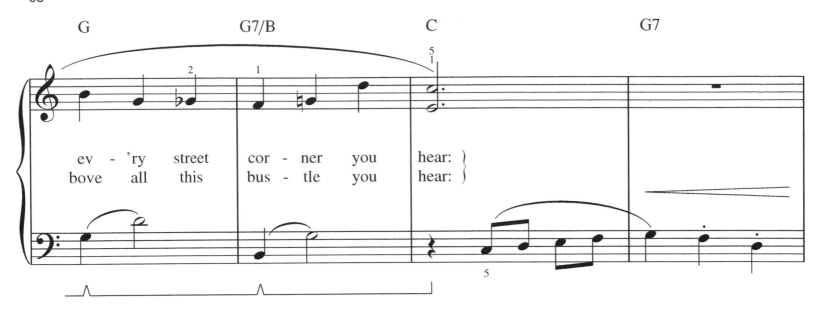

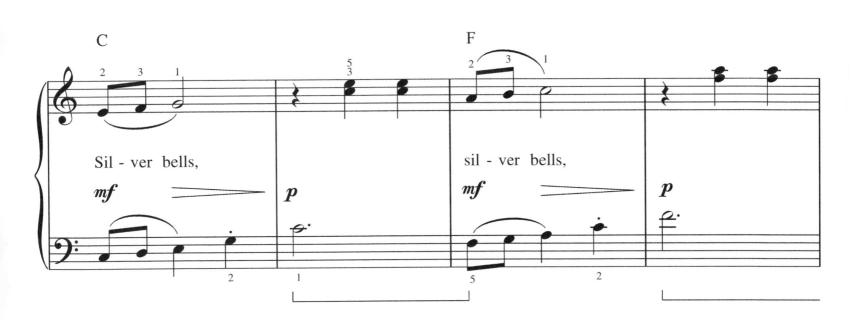

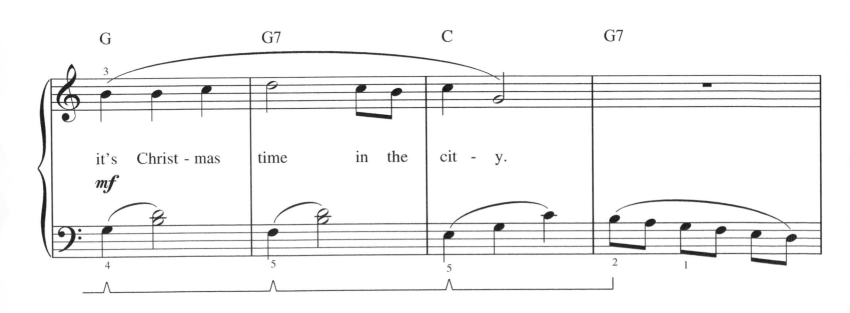

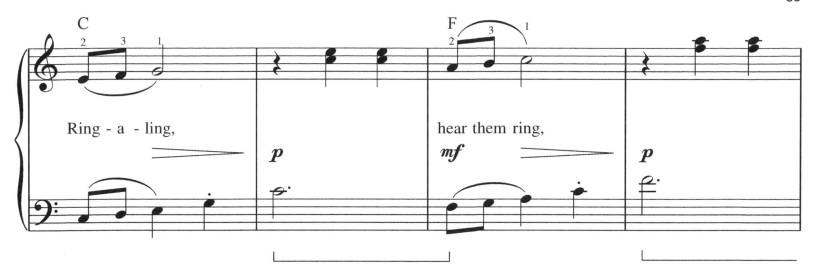

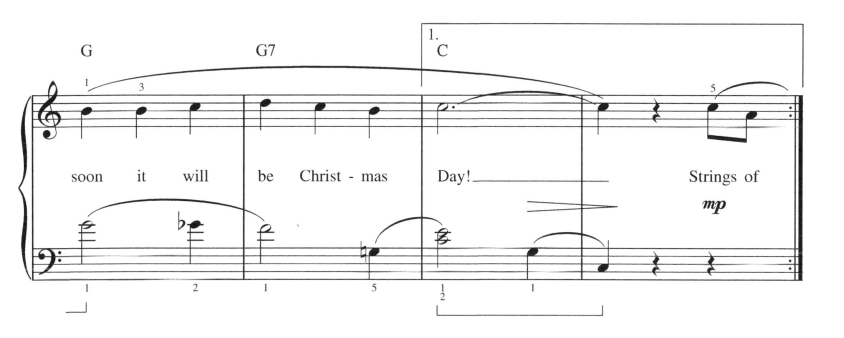

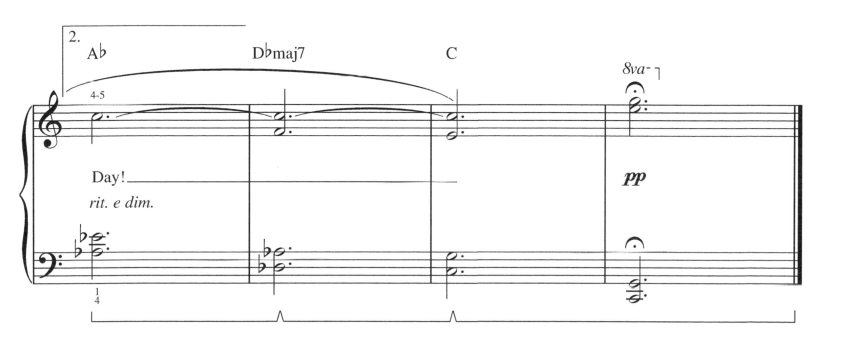

# THIS CHRISTMAS

Words and Music by DONNY HATHAWAY
and NADINE McKINNOR
Arranged by Phillip Keveren

**Moderate Pop Rock**

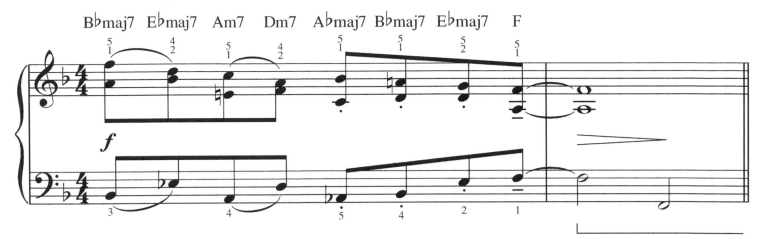

Hang all the mis-tle-toe.___ I'm gon-na get to know you
Pres - ents and cards are here.___ My world is filled with cheer and

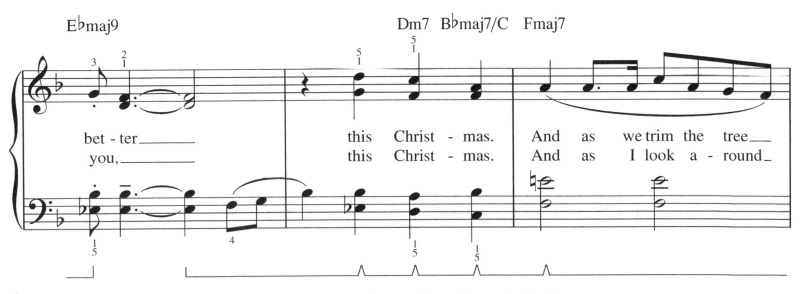

bet - ter___ this Christ - mas. And as we trim the tree___
you,___ this Christ - mas. And as I look a - round___

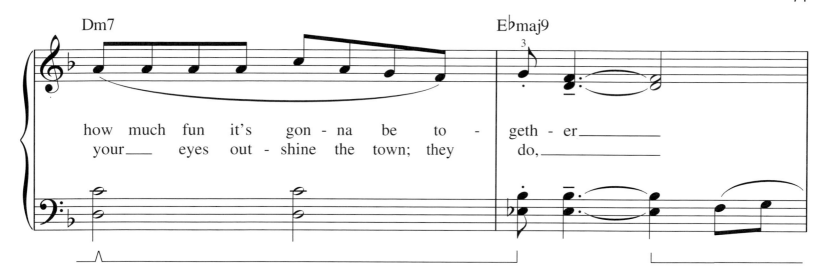

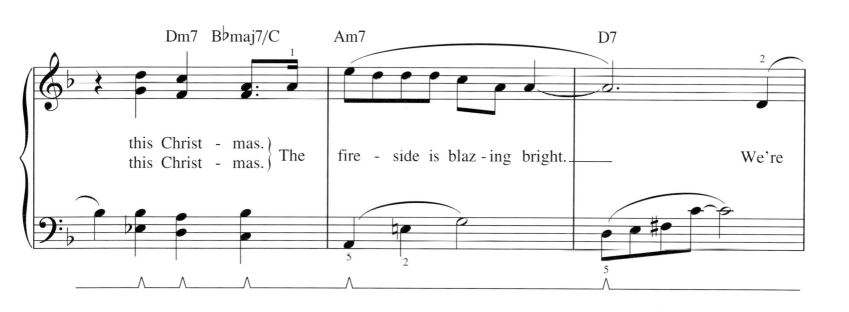

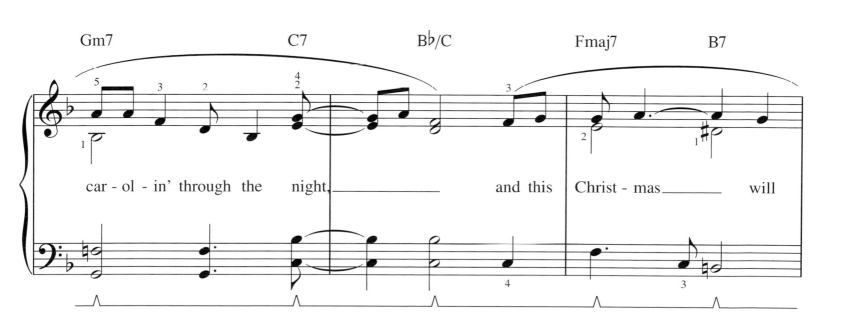

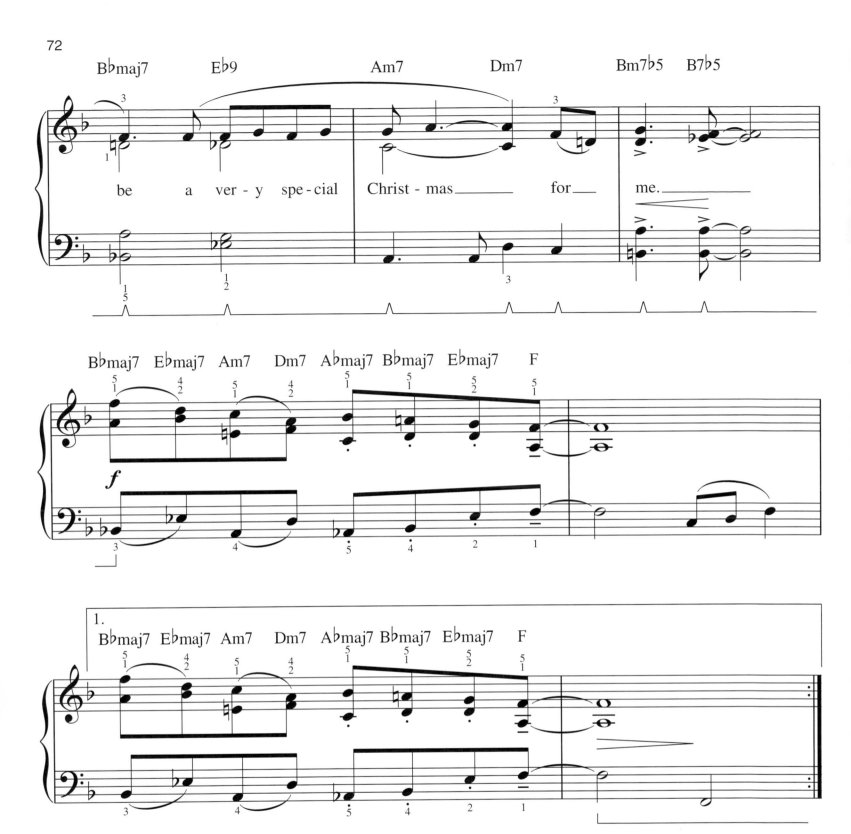